Growing Up with SCIENCE®

Third Edition

14

Spring–Thermography

Marshall Cavendish
Reference
New York

Marshall Cavendish
99 White Plains Road
Tarrytown, NY 10591

www.marshallcavendish.us

© 2006 Marshall Cavendish Corporation
© 1987, 1990 Marshall Cavendish Limited

GROWING UP WITH SCIENCE is a registered trademark
of Marshall Cavendish Corporation

Library of Congress Cataloging-in-Publication Data

Growing up with science.— 3rd ed.
 p. cm.
 Includes index.
 Contents: v. 1. Abrasive-Astronomy — v. 2. Atmosphere-Cable television —
v. 3. Cable travel-Cotton — v. 4. Crane-Electricity — v. 5 Electric motor-
Friction — v. 6. Fuel cell-Immune system — v. 7. Induction-Magnetism —
v. 8. Mapmaking-Mining and quarrying — v. 9. Missile and torpedo-Oil
exploration and refining — v. 10. Optics-Plant kingdom — v. 11. Plasma
physics-Radiotherapy — v. 12. Railroad system-Seismology — v. 13.
Semiconductor-Sports — v. 14. Spring-Thermography — v. 15. Thermometer-
Virus, biological — v. 16. Virus, computer-Zoology — v. 17. Index.
 ISBN 0-7614-7505-2 (set)
 ISBN 0-7614-7519-2 (vol. 14)
 1. Science—Encyclopedias.

Q121.G764 2006
503—dc22

                                                    2004049962
                                   09 08 07 06 05 6 5 4 3 2 1

Printed in China

CONSULTANT

Donald R. Franceschetti, Ph.D.

Dunavant Professor at the University of Memphis

Donald R. Franceschetti is a member of the American
Chemical Society, the American Physical Society, the
Cognitive Science Society, the History of Science Society,
and the Society for Neuroscience.

CONTRIBUTORS TO VOLUME 14

Ian Graham

Emma Young

Marshall Cavendish

Editors: Peter Mavrikis and Susan Rescigno

Editorial Director: Paul Bernabeo

Production Manager: Alan Tsai

The Brown Reference Group

Editors: Leon Gray and Simon Hall

Copy Editor: Lionel Bender

Designer: Sarah Williams

Picture Researchers: Susy Forbes and Laila Torsun

Indexer: Kay Ollerenshaw

Illustrators: Darren Awuah and Mark Walker

Managing Editor: Bridget Giles

Art Director: Dave Goodman

CONTENTS

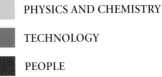

KEY TO COLOR CODING OF ARTICLES

EARTH, SPACE, AND ENVIRONMENTAL SCIENCES

LIFE SCIENCES AND MEDICINE

MATHEMATICS

PHYSICS AND CHEMISTRY

TECHNOLOGY

PEOPLE

Spring

A spring is a device made from an elastic material that can return to its original shape after it has been squeezed or bent. A common example is a steel strip or wire formed into a spiral coil. Springs come in many different shapes and sizes and are often used in machines.

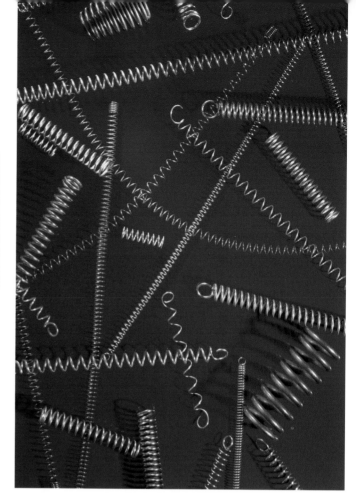

▲ *Springs are made in a variety of shapes and sizes for different applications.*

A physicist might say that a spring is a device for storing energy. The way in which a material can stretch and compress, called elasticity, is clearly a simple and effective way of applying force.

Different solid materials vary greatly in their elasticity. Compare rubber with lead. If it is under pressure, a piece of rubber will spread out to fill a container. When the pressure is removed, the rubber will return quickly to its original shape. A piece of lead, on the other hand, is not elastic. Under enough pressure, it will spread out, but if the pressure is taken away, it still remains flattened. Lead can absorb energy but cannot store it.

Between the extremes of lead and rubber are a number of materials that are elastic to a certain extent, including metals such as copper, steel, and phosphor bronze (normally an alloy of copper, tin, and phosphorus). Their effectiveness as a material for springs may be improved by using different shapes and designs. Metallic springs may take the form of beams, washers, spirals, clips, and so on. The limit of a spring's efficiency is reached when the load on it deforms it permanently, so that it does not regain its original shape. This point is called the elastic limit.

Spring designs

The most common types of springs are metallic spirals. They are flat, shaped like a cylinder, or form some variation of these types, such as tapering cylindrical (conical) or nonflat spiral (volute). A close-coiled cylindrical spring has the coils wound so tightly that they are in contact with each other even in the unloaded state of the spring. This design acts as an extension spring—a door spring is an example. An extension spring stores energy when it is in a stretched-out position. More common is the open-coiled cylindrical spring. It works by means of compression—an example is the spring in a car seat or a mattress.

Flat spiral springs are used in clocks and similar devices. A thin strip of metal is wound into a flat spiral. The outer end of the spiral is fixed to the mechanism. The inner end is shaped to receive the end of a shaft or a key. Twisting the key makes the coils of the spring tighten so that they store energy.

Leaf springs were used in the nineteenth century on horse-drawn and railroad carriages and are still used in the rear suspensions of many vehicles. They consist of a number of springy strips of steel stacked together. The shortest of the lengths (leaf) is placed nearest the source of the load. Some leaf

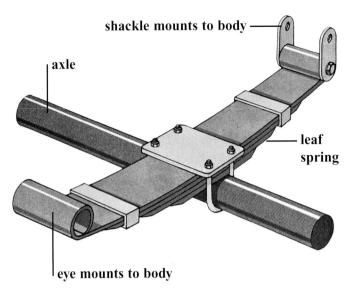

▶ This illustration shows a leaf spring supporting an axle. The axle can move vertically (up and down) but not horizontally (side to side).

shackle mounts to body

axle

leaf spring

eye mounts to body

springs are supported at both ends and carry a central load. Others are fixed at one end and carry a load at the other end.

Lathes are sometimes used to make special-purpose springs in small numbers. Spring wire is fed off a reel. It passes over a former and hits a plate that forces it to coil back around the former. It is then cut off and finished.

Materials

Springs were traditionally made from steel, but they are now made from a wide variety of materials. Some, like titanium, are metals. Others, such as carbon fiber, are nonmetals. Even materials normally thought of as being very brittle, such as ceramics and glass, can be used to make springs. Some springs are even made from liquids or gases. A hydraulic spring is made from a tube full of oil with a piston at one end. A weight pressing down on the piston compresses the oil. An air spring is a metal tube or rubber bag full of air. Its stiffness can be adjusted by pumping more air in or letting some of the air out. Some road vehicles and railroad carriages use air springs to support their weight.

▲ This is a pocket watch dating from 1675. A tightened spring provides the stored energy to drive the watch.

See also: CARBON FIBER • CERAMICS, INDUSTRIAL • ELASTICITY • ENERGY • GLASS

Star

Most of the stars that twinkle in the night sky are great globes of hot gas billions of miles from Earth. Although they appear not to move, stars are in fact rushing headlong through space. There are many different kinds of stars—great supergiants, tiny white dwarfs, variable stars, exploding stars, and stars that cluster together.

Serious study of the stars did not begin until about six thousand years ago. The priests of ancient Babylon, Chaldea, and Egypt first studied the heavens for religious reasons. They believed that the patterns of stars in the sky at the time of a person's birth affected his or her future life.

The priests had another reason for stargazing: they could tell the time of year from the star patterns appearing in the night sky. This feature helped them to plan a calendar, which was a necessity for organizing society. The priests' stargazing also provided the basis of the science of astronomy. The Greek scientist Hipparchus (lived c. 150 BCE) was one of the first real astronomers. He produced the first known star catalog, which was handed down to us by the Egyptian scholar Ptolemy (100–170 CE).

Ancient astronomers believed that all the stars in the night sky lay the same distance away on the inside of a great celestial (heavenly) sphere. The celestial sphere marked the edge of the universe. It rotated (turned) about its center, where Earth was located. Earth was the fixed center of the universe. The rotation of the sphere once a year explained why different stars became visible month by month.

The constellations

The early astronomers soon learned to recognize the patterns made by the brightest stars in the sky. They imagined these patterns formed the shapes of

▲ Stars are grouped together in great galaxies. Many take the shape of large spirals or whirlpools, such as this one, simply called the Whirlpool Galaxy.

animals, gods, heroes, and everyday objects. As a result, these beings and objects became important in the mythology of the early civilizations.

The star patterns are now called constellations. With only minor changes, the constellations appear the same today as they did thousands of years ago. People still know them by the names given to them in ancient times. Prominent constellations include the Great Bear (Big Dipper), the Swan, and the Bull in the Northern Hemisphere, and the Archer, the Serpent, and the Centaur in the Southern Hemisphere. Astronomers call the constellations by their Latin names. In Latin, the Great Bear is Ursa Major, the Swan is Cygnus, the Bull is Taurus, the Archer is Sagittarius, the Serpent is Serpens, and the Centaur is Centaurus. Altogether there are about 88 officially recognized constellations.

Stars within a constellation are usually identified by a Greek letter. Usually, but not always, the brightest star in the constellation is called alpha, the second brightest beta, the third brightest gamma, and so on through the Greek alphabet. Many of the stars in a constellation also have their own names. The brightest star in the constellation Canis Major (the Great Dog), as well as in the entire sky, is called alpha Canis Majoris, or Sirius.

Pinpointing the stars

Locating a star by its position in a constellation is easy if the star and the constellation are clear. It is difficult if the star is dim, and the outline of the constellation is vague. The only sure way to pinpoint a star in the heavens is by some kind of standard reference system.

The system astronomers use is similar to the latitude and longitude grid system used by navigators on Earth. On Earth a ship is located by its latitude (distance north or south of the equator) and longitude (distance east or west of Greenwich, England). In astronomy, a star is also located by north-south and east-west coordinates. These are known as declination and right ascension, respectively. These coordinates pinpoint the stars on the celestial sphere, which is still a good way of picturing the heavens.

The moving stars

As anyone who has looked at the night sky knows, the stars appear to spin overhead during the night. However, it is not that the stars are turning but, rather, Earth that is spinning on its axis. Also, different stars become visible month by month because Earth travels around the Sun during the year.

Although the stars appear to stay in the same places in their constellations century after century, astronomers have discovered that they are actually moving quickly through space. The reason they do not seem to move is that they are so far away from

◄ *This illustration dates from 1761 and shows the Sun at the center of constellations in a celestial sphere. Astrologers believe the positions of the stars and planets influence people and their lives.*

◀ Amateur astronomers observe the night sky through telescopes. It is still possible for amateur astronomers to make important discoveries.

Astronomers have detected a number of stellar objects that lie several billion light years away. This gives an idea of just how large the universe is.

How do astronomers measure such enormous distances? They can measure the distances to a few stars by what is called the parallax method. This method relies on the principle that a nearby object appears to move against a background when viewed from different points. But only a few hundred stars are close enough for this method to work. The distance of most stars must be determined indirectly. This can often be done using known facts or estimates about their apparent and true brightness.

us. Even the closest star, called Proxima Centauri, is over 25 trillion miles (40 trillion kilometers) away. This is so far that it takes light from the star over four years to reach Earth. Astronomers say it is more than four light-years away.

Distances in space are so great that they are often measured in light-years for convenience. Another distance unit astronomers use is the parsec, which is equal to about 3⅓ light-years and is related to the angle Earth's radius subtends in an orbit.

The brightness of stars
On a clear night and far from city lights, one can see more than two thousand stars in the night sky with the naked eye. A few are very bright and are easy to find. Astronomers class them as stars of the first magnitude. Those that are just bright enough to be visible are stars of the sixth magnitude. The other visible stars fall between these two categories.

PROPERTIES AND TYPES OF STARS

Properties of stars		While using up hydrogen		
Mass (compared to Sun)	Lifetime (millions of years)	Brightness (compared to Sun)	Surface temperature (°F and as color)	Example
25	3	80,000	22,220 blue-white	zeta Ophiuchii
16	15	10,000	18,330 blue-white	Spica
6	100	600	9440 white	Regulus
3	500	60	5050 white	Sirius
1.5	2000	6	3660 yellow-white	Altair
1	10,000	1	3100 yellow	Sun
0.8	20,000	0.4	2300 orange	epsilon Eridani

Since the invention of the telescope, the magnitude scale has been extended to cover fainter stars. The largest telescopes can detect stars that are fainter than magnitude 20. The magnitude scale is also extended in the other direction to describe the exceptionally bright stars such as Sirius and Canopus. These have a negative magnitude of −1.45 and −0.73, respectively. On this scale, the Sun has a magnitude of −26.

▼ *Stars are born in vast clouds of gas and dust called nebulae. When a nebula collapses under its own gravity, clumps of matter form. When these become big enough, nuclear reactions begin in their cores and they become stars.*

This magnitude scale relates to a star's brightness as it appears from Earth. It bears no relationship to a star's true brightness because the stars are different distances from Earth. So a very bright star that is far from Earth may look dimmer than a less bright star that is near.

To compare the true brightness of two stars, they must be viewed from the same distance. So astronomers define the true brightness, or absolute magnitude, of a star as the magnitude of the star when viewed at a distance of 33 light-years or 10 parsecs. When classed in this way, two of the brightest stars in the sky are Rigel (magnitude −7) and Betelgeuse (−6).

◀ *This chart shows the characteristics of different types of stars, which determine their "life" and eventual fate.*

Eventual fate		
Expands to become	**Loses outer layers as**	**Core collapses to**
white supergiant	supernova	black hole
yellow supergiant	supernova	neutron star
orange giant	supernova?	neutron star or white dwarf
red giant	planetary nebula	white dwarf
red giant	planetary nebula	white dwarf
red giant	planetary nebula	white dwarf
red giant	planetary nebula	white dwarf

As Earth spins on its axis, the stars appear to move across the sky. Normally, the motion is too slow to notice, but a photograph taken with a long exposure reveals the paths of the stars.

When astronomers can measure the true brightness of a star, they can figure out how far away it is. They find its apparent brightness by observation, and they know that brightness decreases with distance by the inverse square law. (As the distance of a star from Earth doubles, its brightness is reduced by one-quarter.)

The stellar spectrum

How do astronomers find out the true brightness of a star? Like so many other things, they can often find this out by analyzing the light the star emits. They do this in a spectroscope, which is an instrument that splits light into a spectrum. The spectrum produced is, like that of sunlight, crossed by many dark lines. From the nature and position of these spectral lines, astronomers can learn a great deal about a star.

They can calculate the star's brightness and also the temperature of its surface. They can estimate the star's mass and diameter, which varies a great deal from star to star. Great supergiants, such as Betelgeuse, are hundreds of millions of miles across. White dwarfs, such as van Maanen's star in the constellation Pisces, are only a few thousand

miles across. A typical white dwarf is about the same size as Earth but has a mass equivalent to that of the Sun.

Another characteristic astronomers learn from the spectrum of starlight is the speed at which the star is traveling. As can be explained by the Doppler effect, a change in wavelength occurs when a star is moving; the spectral lines of the elements do not appear where they should. Some are shifted toward the blue end of the spectrum, and this "blueshift" indicates that the star is moving toward Earth. A "redshift" means that the star is moving away from Earth.

The Hertzsprung-Russell diagram

Astronomers divide stars into a number of classes according to their spectrum. Most stars fall into seven main spectral classes, named O, B, A, F, G, K, and M. These classes are listed in order of decreasing surface temperature.

When the spectral class (temperature) of a star is plotted on a graph against the star's absolute brightness (luminosity), definite patterns emerge. Most stars lie within a broad band of decreasing brightness and surface temperature known as the main sequence. The stars move across, off, and back to the main sequence over time. Astronomers refer to the graph as the Hertzsprung-Russell diagram, named for the two people who first devised it.

Stellar life and death

A star is born from a nebula (cloud) of hydrogen gas and dusty material in space. This material gradually coalesces under gravity and forms a rotating ball. The ball collapses under gravity, and heats up under the energy of the collapse. Eventually, at temperatures of 10 to 15 million degrees Fahrenheit (5.5 to 8 million degrees Celsius), the hydrogen atoms in the star's core begin to fuse, producing enough energy to make the star shine. The star continues to shine for several billion years until its hydrogen is used up. Then it expands into a huge red giant, before collapsing and getting smaller and smaller until it becomes a white dwarf.

White dwarfs are bodies about the size of Earth. They consist of matter that is incredibly dense. One tablespoonful of such matter would weigh several tons. White dwarfs represent the final stage in the complete life cycle of a star such as the Sun.

Stars much more massive than the Sun have a lot more hydrogen, but they use it up faster. Stars up to one hundred times the mass of the Sun burn up their hydrogen so quickly that they grow into huge supergiants in perhaps 10 to 12 million years. They then blow up in a fantastic explosion called a supernova. During the explosion, the outer layers of matter in the star are blasted into space. The remaining core collapses on itself to form a tiny body consisting entirely of neutrons.

This neutron star is millions of times more dense than a white dwarf and typically measures only about 10 miles (16 kilometers) across. It rotates

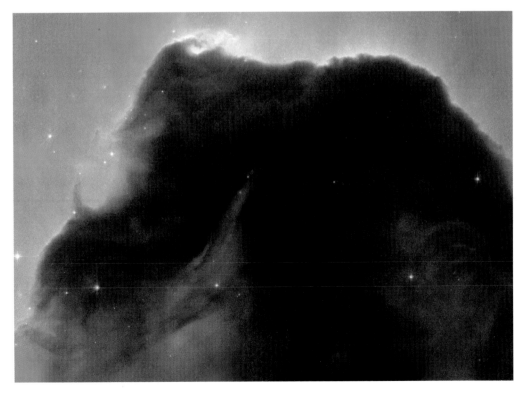

▶ *This vast dark cloud of cosmic dust is known as the Horsehead Nebula because of its shape. The dust is seen against the background of a bright cloud of gas lit up by nearby stars.*

rapidly and emits beams of light and other radiation from its north and south poles. If one of the beams sweeps past Earth, the star appears to flash on and off. This aspect gives it an alternative name—a pulsar. The fastest pulsars spin almost one thousand times a second. Gradually, they slow down over millions of years as they radiate energy into space. The slowest pulsars discovered so far spin once every 8.5 seconds or so.

A well-known pulsar is located in the Crab Nebula in the constellation Taurus. This pulsar is the remains of a supernova explosion that occurred in 1054 CE and was recorded by Chinese astronomers. The cloud of gas and dust hurled out by the explosion is now about six light-years across and still expanding.

Black holes, novas, and variable stars

A more massive star has an even more extraordinary end. Its core continues to collapse beyond

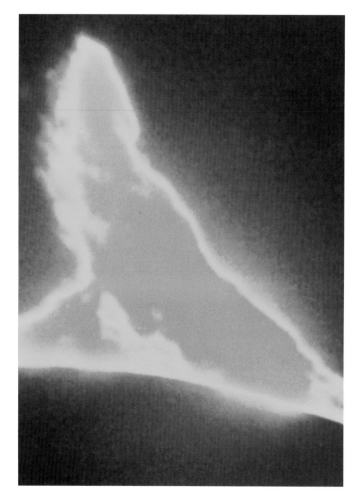

The Sun shines because its center is like a hydrogen bomb exploding in slow motion. It is now about halfway through its life, so it should keep shining for another five billion years.

the neutron star stage. It forms a body known as a black hole, in which gravity is so strong that nothing, not even light, can escape from it. Although black holes are invisible, astronomers can find them by looking for the effect their immense force of gravity has on nearby matter.

Some stars undergo a less shattering explosion than a supernova. They suddenly flare up to about ten thousand times their usual brightness. Astronomers call them novas. Whereas supernovas are seen very rarely, two or three novas can be seen every year in Earth's part of the sky.

Many other stars vary in brightness more gradually over periods of days, weeks, or years. They vary in brightness not because they explode, but because, for example, they are getting larger or smaller. Many types of variable stars are found.

The Cepheids are variable stars that change in brightness periodically, from more than once a day to every 70 days or so. Cepheid variable stars are named after Delta Cephei, which is a star in the constellation Cepheus. It was the first of this type of star to be discovered. Its variability was first observed as long ago as 1784. Mira, also called Omicron Ceti, is a variable star in the constellation Cetus with a much longer period—some 332 days.

Companion stars

Other stars appear to be variable, but they are not. Algol in the constellation Perseus is a star of this type, called an eclipsing binary. It actually consists

◄ *The surface of a star like the Sun is a boiling mass of fiery hot gas. Vast explosions send solar flares curling out thousands of miles into space. Cooler darker spots appear from time to time, caused by intense magnetic disturbances.*

of two stars—a bright one and a dim one—that orbit each other. Seen from Earth, they periodically pass in front of each other, eclipsing each other. When the dim star passes in front of the bright star, the brightness of the system falls.

There are many binary (double) star systems like this. But only a few can be seen eclipsing one another. Many binary stars can be seen in a low-powered telescope; others cannot be told apart. Other stars have more than one companion. They are called multiple stars. The bright star Alpha Centauri in the constellation Centaurus is a triple star system. The star Castor in the constellation Gemini consists of six parts. There appear to be considerably more binary and multiple stars than there are single stars such as the Sun.

DID YOU KNOW?

When the first pulsar was discovered in 1967 by British scientist Jocelyn Bell-Burnell (1943–), it was nicknamed "LGM1" (meaning "Little Green Men 1"). Scientists wondered if its regular bursts of radio energy of 0.05 seconds duration, every 1.3 seconds, might be a signal sent by intelligent beings from another world. However, the discovery of more pulsars in different parts of the sky suggested they were caused by natural phenomena, not messages from extraterrestrials.

On a rather larger scale, stars also cluster together in loose groups and form what are called open clusters. The most famous cluster is the Pleiades in the constellation Taurus. It is often called the Seven Sisters because many people can make out its seven brightest stars with the naked eye, but telescopes reveal about five hundred stars.

Open clusters contain at most only a few hundred stars. A different kind of star cluster, called a globular cluster, resembles a great globe containing thousands of stars. The grouping of stars can be taken even further. All the stars in space

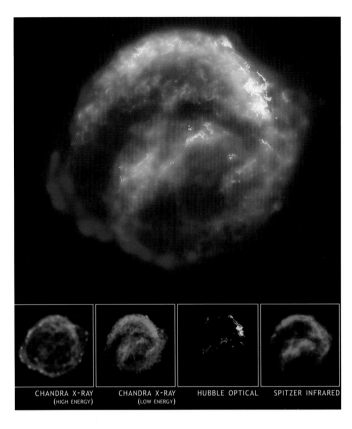

CHANDRA X-RAY (HIGH ENERGY)   CHANDRA X-RAY (LOW ENERGY)   HUBBLE OPTICAL   SPITZER INFRARED

▲ *When a giant star suddenly explodes as a supernova, it can outshine a galaxy. Three different NASA observatories—from X-rays to infrared light—took these views of a supernova explosion.*

group together into galaxies (great star islands) with more or less empty space between them. On a larger scale, the galaxies themselves group together. The Milky Way galaxy is part of a cluster of galaxies called the Local Group. It contains about 20 galaxies. In the constellation Virgo, there is a cluster of about 2,500 galaxies, called the Virgo cluster, measuring more than 50 million light-years across.

On a yet larger scale, clusters of galaxies group together to form superclusters that travel through space together. The Virgo cluster is at the center of one supercluster, called the Local Supercluster. It contains about one hundred groups and clusters of galaxies and is 200 million light-years across.

See also: ASTRONOMY • BLACK HOLE • DOPPLER EFFECT • ECLIPSE • MASS AND WEIGHT • NAVIGATION • SPECTROSCOPY • SUN • TELESCOPE • UNIVERSE

Statistics

Statistics is the mathematics of collecting, analyzing, and interpreting large amounts of data. Once the data are organized, it is much easier to understand them, see patterns and trends within them, and draw conclusions from these. People use statistics to analyze data in all areas of life, from insurance and crime to business and science.

▲ *The results of elections are analyzed statistically to discover how people vote according to their age, sex, and many other factors.*

The science of statistics draws conclusions from facts collected by surveys, experiments, tests, questionnaires, and other methods that are helpful to a wide variety of groups. Business, manufacturing, advertising, insurance, public opinion polls, and governments all use statistics to identify patterns and trends, help make them more efficient, and make predictions.

For example, a government often needs to know the size of its country's population and how it is composed with regard to age, income, and family size. This information helps in planning for future needs in food production, roads, schools, hospitals, and homes. So a census is taken—a listing of every individual in the country that includes age, sex, occupation, and other personal details.

Completed census forms alone would be useless to the government. So statisticians organize the material and present it in the form of tables that show not only the total population, but also the numbers in different age groups and particular occupations, at various income levels and stages of education, and so on. Departments of the government need this kind of information to plan their programs and services.

Scientists also need statistics to help them deal with the masses of facts and figures produced by experiments. For example, a new drug must undergo many tests during its development. The results are analyzed statistically to see if the drug is safe and useful. In space science, information sent to Earth by satellites and space probes is analyzed statistically. In 1992, a satellite called COBE provided important evidence about the origin of the universe. Data collected by COBE were used to produce maps of the sky. The maps showed ripples that were said to be evidence of structures in the early universe. In fact, features in the original maps were at the same level as unwanted "noise" caused by the electronics in the detecting system. The scientists used statistical analysis to reveal the ripples hidden in the noise. The evidence came not from the maps, but from the statistics.

Branches of statistics

Some sciences make such an extensive use of statistics that they have developed a particular branch of statistics. Biostatistics is a branch of statistics used in biology. Chemometrics is the use of statistical methods in chemistry. Demography is a branch of statistics that looks at populations. Other branches of statistics are applied to economics, engineering, and physics.

Finding averages

Averages are often needed—for example, the average weight of a group of people, the average age of a population, or the average number of people who read newspapers. Averages give an idea of the middle amount of something.

But there are different kinds of averages. With a class of 20 children, their average age is found by adding up their various ages and dividing by the number of children (20). This type of average is called an arithmetical average or arithmetical mean. If all the children's ages were arranged from

▼ *In games of chance, statisticians can calculate the probability of a card of a particular suit or value being dealt.*

the lowest to the highest, the age exactly in the middle would be called the median, another kind of average. The age of most of the children in the class is called the mode, the third kind of average. Statisticians must decide which type of average they want to use and which one is most suited to their purpose.

Showing statistics visually

An interesting way to look at statistics is in the form of a graph. For example, to graph the age data in the class of 20 children, the various ages of the children in the class would be listed in one column. The number of children of each age would fill a second column. This data can then be used to plot a graph. It would be a frequency-distribution type of graph because it would show the number of times (frequency) a particular age occurs. Some frequency curves are shaped like a bell. They are called normal curves or distributions. Many data give normal curves, such as heights of people,

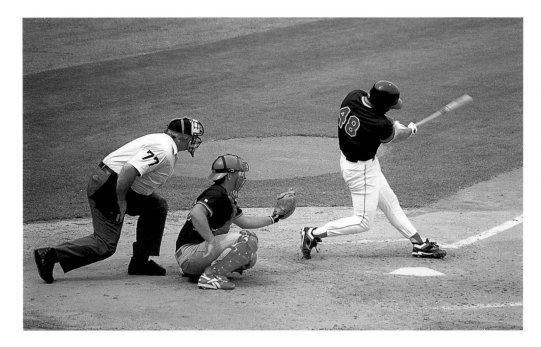

◄ *A Boston Red Sox baseball player in practice at Fort Myers, Florida. Statistics of such sports as baseball are followed avidly by fans. They provide a way of presenting a team's performance that can be compared easily to other teams.*

scores on IQ tests, or the number of times "heads" appears when a coin is tossed many times. The data of children's ages could also be shown on a bar graph or histogram. In a histogram, blocks or columns are used to represent the number of times each age appears. The information could also be displayed on a pie chart, where a circular "pie" is cut into portions, with the size of each portion showing the percentage of children of a particular age.

Computers can present statistical information in novel and visually exciting ways that make the information easier to understand. They can produce three-dimensional presentations and animated graphics. For example, computer-generated climate models can create moving maps to show how temperatures might change in different parts of the world in the future.

DID YOU KNOW?

The word *statistics* comes from the Latin word *statisticus*, meaning "to do with state affairs." Statistics originally described the collection and analysis of data about the state. By the early nineteenth century, it came to mean the general collection and analysis of data.

Probability theory

Probability theory predicts how likely it is that a particular event will happen. The event could be something as straightforward as whether a team will win or lose a game or whether a tossed coin will land heads or tails. When tossed once, a coin is just as likely to land heads as it is to land tails. So there is a 50 percent chance that it will land heads and a 50 percent chance that it will land tails.

If the coin is tossed 100 times, it would be expected to come up heads 50 times and tails 50 times. But it could land heads 100 times. That result is not impossible, just very unlikely. To get 99 heads and 1 tail, even though this is still unlikely, is slightly more probable than getting 100 heads. Plotting all the different combinations of heads and tails on a graph would produce the bell-shaped graph of a normal curve.

When meteorologists prepare a weather forecast, they may not be able to say that it will definitely rain in a particular place, but they can give the probability of rain for an area. When they say, "It will not rain tomorrow," they really mean the probability of rain is so low that it is not worth mentioning. Weather forecasts are prepared with the help of computers. The computers apply statistical analysis to vast amounts of data from satellites and surface weather stations. They create models of the world's weather. These models are constantly compared with the actual weather and modified to make them more accurate. They help calculate the probability of rain, storms, or settled weather in the coming days.

Probability theory is used in statistics to explain the results of checking the quality of a mass-produced product, such as a brand of shampoo. A small group of bottles is chosen at random from each batch that is produced. If the shampoo in this sample selection is up to standard, then there is a high probability that the entire batch will be of the same quality. This is known as random sampling.

Some probabilities are called conditional probabilities because they have certain conditions that must be obeyed first. Suppose, for example, you were asked to draw a single card from a pack of 52. What would the chance be that it was the six of hearts? It would be 1 in 52 because all the cards in the pack are equally likely to be drawn and so they all have the same probability. But if a card was drawn, and you were told it was a heart, what would the probability be of it being the six of hearts? There are 13 hearts in a pack of cards, so the probability in this case is 1 in 13. This is a conditional probability because the probability of a card being the six of hearts is conditional on it being known to be a heart.

Crime statistics

Police often use statistics to help them figure out the size of police force that is needed in a particular area and where to concentrate that force. A count is made of the numbers and types of crimes in an area. When the results are analyzed statistically, the police can see whether certain types of crime are increasing, whether they need more recruits, and whether they are giving their police officers the correct type of training.

Are you the correct weight?

The insurance field is another area in which the use of statistics is very important. A person who takes out insurance on his or her life does so to provide

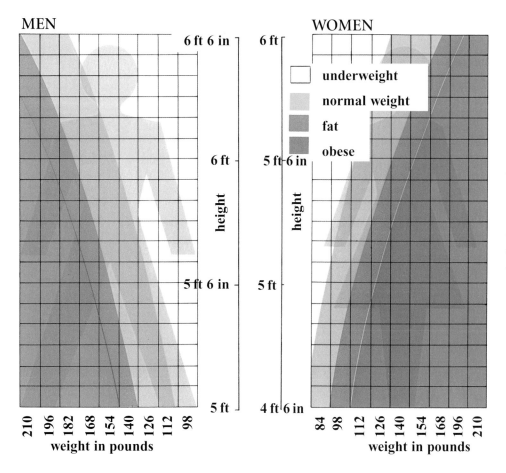

◀ *These charts show roughly how much an adult should weigh according to his or her height. They are based on the weights of a large number of people and then averaged statistically. If a person's weight falls in the white area, he or she is underweight; in the yellow area, normal; in the red area, fat; and in the blue area, obese.*

DID YOU KNOW?

The most number of babies born during one pregnancy was ten. Unfortunately, most of the babies from this pregnancy died. The most number of babies born who survived is seven (called septuplets). Septuplets were born in November 1997 to a woman in Iowa. Another set of septuplets was born to a woman in Saudi Arabia in January 1998.

money for his or her family in the event of the person's death. To keep up the insurance policy, the insured person must pay the insurance company a regular amount, called a premium. It may be paid monthly, every three months, or on a yearly basis.

To figure out the amount an individual will have to pay, the insurance company uses tables of statistics. They take into account the person's age, height, weight, and habits. Statistical tables will tell them the average life span of people who match the insured person in age, physical condition, and habits, such as whether they smoke or not, drink or not, and so on. The insurance company then figures out the amount of the premium that will have to be paid on that insurance policy.

A person who smokes or is very overweight must pay higher premiums because that person is more likely to die sooner. If a man is 25 pounds (11 kilograms) overweight, his life expectancy will be reduced by 25 percent. But a slim nonsmoker who does not drink and gets plenty of exercise will pay a lower premium. A person who compiles statistics of births, deaths, illnesses, and accidents for insurance companies, using them to calculate risks and insurance premiums, is called an actuary. Actuaries are highly trained mathematicians.

▶ *Health and age statistics reveal the ways in which the health of different age groups in a population change over time. This information is then used to plan health education campaigns, for example, about the dangers of smoking cigarettes or drinking alcohol, and the provision of health services.*

Having babies

When a woman becomes pregnant, there is roughly a 50 percent chance she will have a boy and a 50 percent chance she will have a girl. But some women have more than one baby during one pregnancy. Statistically, the birth of twins can be expected only once in every 50 to 150 pregnancies. But this figure depends on the ethnic origins of the parents. Black women have the highest number of twins and Asian women the lowest. Triplets are born about once in every 8,000 pregnancies, and quadruplets (four babies) are born only about once in 700,000 pregnancies.

Some statistics also record infant mortality—the number of babies who die soon after birth. In the developed countries, this number is comparatively low. But in the developing world, it is especially high. Many of the mothers do not get enough food to eat, and the babies are often born small and weak. The babies may also not be getting enough nourishment from their mothers after they are born, or they may die from diseases that are no longer present in developed countries. Even in developed countries, however, doctors are trying to reduce the infant mortality rate. They are persuading mothers to go for more checkups during pregnancy and are providing better health-care for babies after birth.

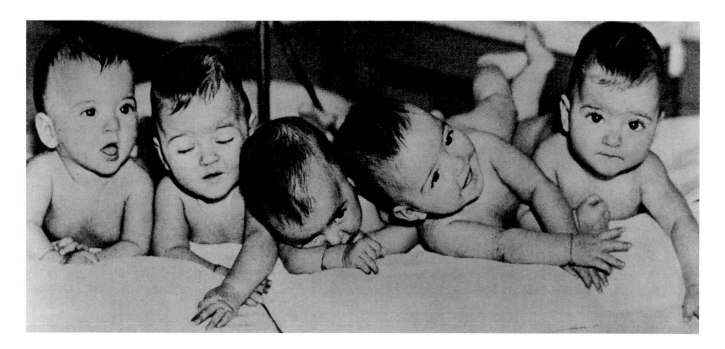

The census

A census is a count of the population. In ancient Rome, lists were prepared of people and their property, mainly so that they could be taxed, and the men could be called up as soldiers. These were the first statistics. In 1066 in England, the advisors of William the Conqueror (1027–1087) made a famous census of people, land, and property that was listed in the *Domesday Book*. Originally, censuses were taken by governments just as a way of

▲ *Statisticians use birth and population statistics to calculate how often multiple births are likely to occur. Insurance companies are interested in this information because some families now take out insurance policies to protect themselves from the financial burden of a multiple birth—in this case, quintuplets.*

counting the number of people in a population, but now censuses gather much more information. They can tell governments about housing needs, age, employment, income, race, and sex of people. Plans and policies can then be drawn up and implemented to counteract unfavorable trends.

Today, most national censuses are taken once every ten years. With modern computers, statistics from the census can be compiled much more quickly than before so that census material is no longer out of date before it can be analyzed.

◄ *This is Pascal's triangle. The numbers within the triangle are arranged so that they can be used to calculate statistical probabilities. For example, the third horizontal row shows the odds of likely numbers of boys or girls in a family of three children. The numbers add up to eight. The least likely combinations of all girls or all boys are given by the end figures, giving odds of one in eight.*

See also: CALCULATOR • COMPUTER

Steam engine

A steam engine uses steam to drive a piston back and forth. This piston action can then be used to drive other machines. Steam engines are best known for their use in powering locomotives, but they were once used for many other purposes.

The first commercially successful steam engine was built by English blacksmith Thomas Newcomen (1663–1729). Newcomen earned his living as a hardware dealer in Dartmouth, England, where he was in partnership with English inventor John Calley, also known as John Cawley (1685–1729). He may have known about the model engine built by French inventor Denis Papin (1647–1712). In Papin's drawing, the piston was moved by steam. Newcomen also knew about the water pump of English engineer Thomas Savery (1650–1715), which was powered by steam.

Newcomen and Calley went into partnership with Savery and built their first steam engine in 1712. It was used to pump water out of flooded mines in the coal-mining area of Staffordshire, England.

Newcomen's steam engine is based on the scientific law that when steam cools down and condenses (becomes water again), its volume is greatly reduced. If the cooling and condensing is carried out inside a sealed container, it creates a vacuum. Newcomen made the sealed container a large cylinder set upright, open at the top, and with a circular piston that moved up and down. The cylinder below the piston was filled with steam, which was condensed in the same container by a spray of cold water released into it. The vacuum forced the piston to move downward. This forceful movement is called a working stroke.

Newcomen's steam engine was very slow and did not produce a great deal of power, but it was the best means of pumping water out of mines available at that time. As a result, it was widely used in Britain for many years.

◄ When water is heated until it boils, the liquid vaporizes and becomes steam. The steam jets out of a kettle spout because it takes up much more space than water. The force of this expansion is used by steam engines to do work.

▶ *Thomas Newcomen's steam engine at Dudley Castle, as shown in an engraving by Barney from 1719. Newcomen's engines were used to pump water out of mines and to raise water to power waterwheels.*

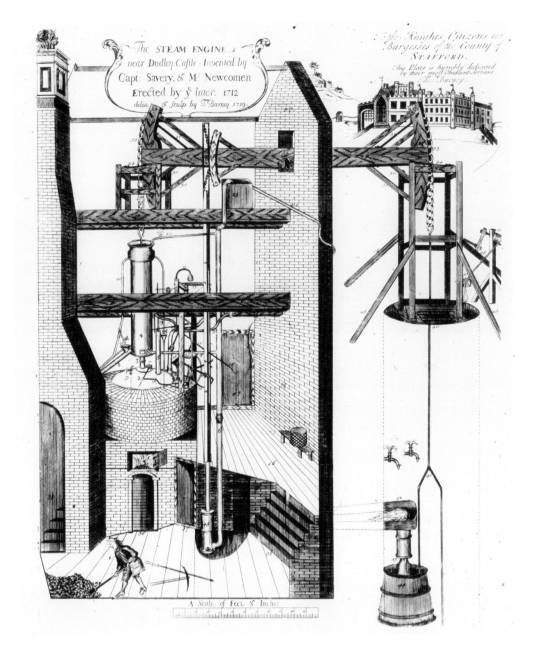

Some engineers of the mid-nineteenth century tried to make the Newcomen engine drive different kinds of machinery, instead of using it only for operating pumps. For example, John Oxley in 1763 installed a Newcomen engine with a ratchet (toothed) wheel to turn a shaft and lift loads of coal from a mine.

Watt's steam engine

Scottish engineer James Watt (1736–1819) got his idea for a steam engine while repairing a model of a Newcomen engine. In the Newcomen engine, steam was condensed in the same cylinder as the piston. Watt realized that this wasted a great deal of heat because the cylinder had to be heated over and over again. All the heat was then lost every time it was cooled to allow condensation.

Watt's idea was to install a separate condenser, which he connected to the piston by a valve. The condenser could be kept cool at the same time as the cylinder could be kept hot. This produced a 75 percent saving in fuel. Watt patented his steam engine in 1769.

Like Newcomen's engine, Watt's engine was used mainly to drive pumps. In 1780, Watt started to use a system of gears to make a rotary engine. The

acting engine. This improvement not only gave the engine twice as much power, but also made it run more smoothly and use less fuel.

Trevithick's engine

English engineer Richard Trevithick (1771–1833) set himself the task of making a boiler strong enough to withstand high pressure. Trevithick built a small cylindrical boiler, which he mounted inside a larger boiler. He discovered that this would withstand steam pressure up to 50 pounds per square inch (3.5 kilograms per square centimeter).

Trevithick designed the flue—a pipe that carries flames and hot gases inside the boiler—in the shape of a "U." It ran the length of one side of the boiler and back along the other side. The fire was at one end, and a chimney was at the other. This created a strong, compact boiler. The engine fueled by this

▲ *The steam locomotives of English engineer Robert Stephenson (1803–1859) successfully harnessed the power of high-pressure steam. They were the first practical steam locomotives capable of doing useful and prolonged work.*

rotation was created by connecting a rod from the piston to a crank. In designing this new system, Watt developed the flywheel, which is a heavy wheel that has its greatest weight around the outer edge. The flywheel helps steady the turning movement in steam-powered machines.

In 1783, Watt discovered how to make the upward movement a working stroke, as well as the downward movement. This is known as a double-

▶ *This diagram shows the cycle of a single-acting steam engine. It uses the expansion of steam (1) to push a piston to the end of a cylinder (2). This in turn pushes a crankshaft and flywheel (3). The momentum of the turning flywheel then pushes the piston back to its original position (4).*

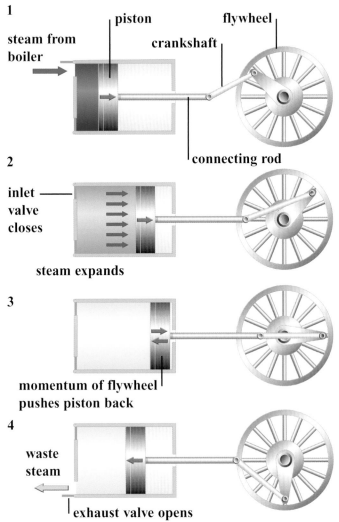

1
steam from boiler
piston
crankshaft
flywheel
connecting rod

2
inlet valve closes
steam expands

3
momentum of flywheel pushes piston back

4
waste steam
exhaust valve opens

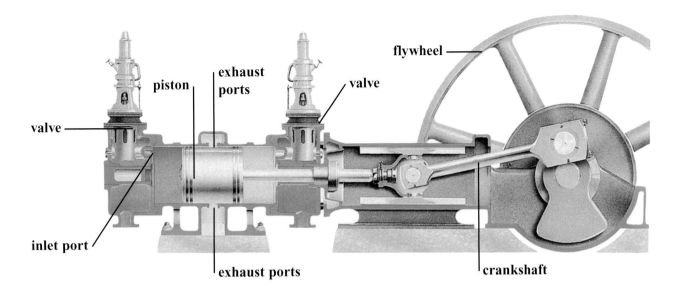

▲ This illustration of a double-acting uniflow engine shows the two exhaust ports in the middle of the cylinder that are covered and uncovered by the moving piston.

boiler could also be made smaller. A reduction in size made it possible to think of using steam power for road transportation.

In 1801, Trevithick built the first full-size steam carriage, but it performed poorly. He then turned to railroads. In 1804, he built the world's first locomotive for the Penydarren Ironworks in South Wales. Four years later, he built the locomotive called *Catch-Me-Who-Can*. It was used for pleasure rides near Euston Square in London, which is now the site of one of London's main railroad stations.

How a steam engine works

A steam engine is an external combustion engine, which means the fuel is burned outside the engine. Most steam engines are double-acting. Steam is first allowed into one end of the cylinder. The piston is pushed forward by the steam, and the inlet port at that end of the cylinder is closed by a valve. The steam trapped behind the piston then expands, pushing the piston toward the other end of the cylinder. This opens the exhaust valve, allowing the steam to escape. Then exactly the same process takes place at the other end of the cylinder so that the piston is pushed back to complete the cycle. If

the steam engine is to be used for pumping or hammering, the back-and-forth movement of the piston can be used directly. In the steam engines used to power ships or locomotives, the back-and-forth movement must be changed to a rotary (round-and-round) movement. This is done by attaching a connecting rod to the end of the piston rod and then attaching the other end of the connecting rod to a drive wheel or heavy flywheel, using a crankshaft.

Compound steam engines

Compound steam engines have two or more cylinders. The steam first goes into a small, high-pressure cylinder. The exhaust steam from here is then taken into a large, low-pressure cylinder.

DID YOU KNOW?

Steam cars were once very popular. The most successful models were designed by twins Francis Edgar Stanley (1849–1918) and Freelan Oscar Stanley (1849–1940) in the United States. Over 60,000 Stanley steam cars were built between 1897 and 1927. A Stanley steam car broke the world speed record in 1906, with a speed of 127 miles (204 kilometers) per hour.

◄ *Power station workers repair a steam turbine. Steam turbines drive the electricity generators in most of the world's power stations. Steam made in the power station's boilers by heat from burning fuel spins a turbine at high speed. The turbine shaft is connected to a generator.*

Triple-expansion steam engines have also been built, with a high-pressure cylinder, a larger intermediate-pressure cylinder, and one or two even larger low-pressure cylinders. There have even been quadruple-expansion engines. Triple- and quadruple-expansion steam engines were used in many oceangoing ships in the early part of the twentieth century.

Boilers

In the early days of steam engines, it was difficult to make a boiler with a large enough heating surface to get heat into the boiling water efficiently. Most of the heat energy produced by burning the fuel went straight up the chimney. Fire-tube boilers improved on these early boilers. In the fire-tube boiler, hot gases from the furnace pass through many small tubes immersed in the water. These hot tubes heat the water and convert it into steam. Steam locomotives use this type of boiler.

The water-tube boiler has many small tubes that contain the water. These tubes pass through the hot combustion chamber, and the water is heated to steam inside the tubes. This design produces steam at a higher pressure. It is usually used to supply steam for steam turbines.

Steam locomotives

The steam locomotive is the best-known use of the steam engine. Hot gases produced by burning coal in a firebox pass through fire tubes and give up their heat to water surrounding the tubes. The steam produced then passes into the cylinders, where it drives the pistons. Connecting rods then pass this movement to the drivewheels. These engines are inefficient, however, as a lot of heat is wasted. When working at full power, ash and cinders are often shot out of the chimney, which also adds to the problems of pollution.

Steam turbines

Steam can be used to power steam turbines. The steam is directed onto a set of blades attached to a rotor. The rotor is like a windmill, with the blades being blown around by the flow of steam.

Steam turbines are commonly used in power stations to drive electricity generators and are also used in large oceangoing vessels to power the propeller or drive an electric motor.

See also: INTERNAL COMBUSTION ENGINE • PROPELLER • STIRLING ENGINE • TURBINE • VALVE

Stirling engine

The Stirling engine was invented before its time. If the correct metals and sealing materials had been available in the 1800s, the Stirling engine would probably have become as popular as the steam engine and the internal combustion engine.

The Stirling engine was invented by Scottish clergyman Robert Stirling (1790–1878) in 1816. He was inspired by the problems and dangers of developing high-pressure steam engines, and he set out to design an efficient engine that would work without the need for a high-pressure boiler. His idea was a good one, and it could have been one answer to the pollution and noise made by other steam engines.

At the time, there were not suitable materials that could stand the high temperatures or that did not wear away or rust easily. Therefore, the Stirling engine could not match the reliability of the steam engine and the internal combustion engine, which, although far more wasteful of power and much dirtier, were more popular.

How the engine works

The Stirling engine is also called an air engine. In the engine cylinder, a piston is driven by first heating, and then cooling, air. A burner at the top heats the walls of the cylinder. The heat is passed through the cylinder to air in a space underneath.

As the hot air expands, it pushes down a displacer (hot air piston), which has a long shank (leg) that passes through a power output piston (cold air piston). When the displacer reaches the power output piston, it pushes it down, too. The ends of both pistons are linked to cogwheels and to each other.

▶ *This is a replica of one of the first hot-air engines to work on the Stirling cycle.*

As the wheels turn, they drive up the displacer, which pushes the hot air out of the hot space and through a chamber called a heat regenerator, which is filled with wire gauze mesh. In the heat regenerator, the air gives up much of its heat and passes into the cold space. The cold air shrinks and draws up the power output piston. This action forces the cold air back up through the heat regenerator, where it is warmed. The warm air enters the hot space, where it is reheated and expanded, and the cycle starts all over again.

Uses of the Stirling engine

Many forms of the Stirling engine were made to drive heavy machinery such as pumps, crushers, and grinders. Four versions of the engine were made to power a transatlantic ship, the *Caloric*, in 1852. Although Stirling engines were more efficient than the early steam engines, the cylinders tended to burn out at the hot end, and they fell out of favor with industrial designers.

Now, with harder metals and other new materials, new designs of the engine are being created, such as the thermomechanical generator.

The thermomechanical generator

The thermomechanical generator was designed to have as few moving parts as possible. Those parts of the engine that are moveable only move slightly. The displacer piston is hung in the cylinder and attached by a flat circular spring to the engine body. The piston does not touch the cylinder, and the space between the cylinder and the cylinder walls is the hot space. A small burner heats the bottom of the cylinder, which in turn heats the gas (helium) in the hot space. This expands and pushes the displacer up about ¹⁄₁₀ inch (0.25 centimeters). The gas enters the cold space above the piston. Above the cold space is a metal diaphragm that acts as the output power piston.

Above the diaphragm is an alternating current (AC) electrical generator. The armature from the generator is fixed to the diaphragm. As the armature is first pulled and then pushed from the electrical generator magnets, it pulls and pushes the

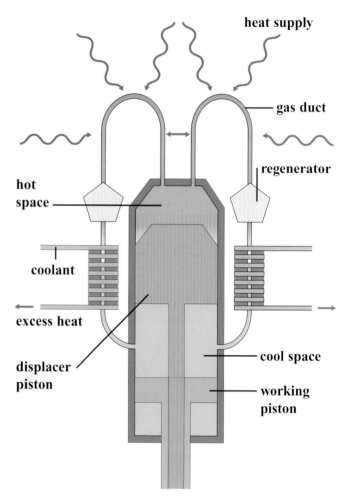

▲ *A Stirling engine consists of two pistons (the displacer piston and the working piston) that move up and down a single, sealed cylinder filled with air.*

diaphragm. As cold air is pushed in and sucked out of the cold space beneath the diaphragm, it moves up and down so that with both forces acting on the armature, the action is almost effortless.

Since the thermomechanical generator has almost no moving parts and therefore needs no oiling and starts as soon as the burner is lit, it has been seen as the ideal engine for producing electricity in remote places such as lighthouses and weather stations.

See also: AUTOMOBILE • GENERATOR • INTERNAL COMBUSTION ENGINE • STEAM ENGINE • WATER

Streetcar and bus

Streetcars and buses are vehicles for transporting people in towns and cities. Streetcars are powered by electricity and run on metal wheels along tracks in the road. Buses run on wheels with rubber tires and are mainly powered by diesel engines.

The world's first streetcars were built in New York in 1832. They ran on a transportation system 1 mile (1.6 kilometers) long called the New York and Harlem Railroad. These early streetcars were pulled by horses and were sometimes known as horse cars. The idea of streetcar transportation became very popular. By the 1880s, there were more than 18,000 horse-drawn streetcars in the United States and more than 3,000 miles (4,830 kilometers) of track. Streetcars were more popular than horse-drawn buses (which ran on wheels rather than tracks) because they gave a smoother ride. By the 1850s, streetcars had spread to Europe and in some places were called trams.

Cable cars

The next stage in the development of the streetcar was to find another way of powering it. Steam was tried first, but early experiments were not very successful. Then the cable car was invented. It was powered by steam engines housed in a building at one end of the streetcar route. The engines drove cables that ran through slots in the road surface. The car had an attachment that went through the slot and gripped the cable. As the cable moved, the car moved. Cable cars were introduced in San Francisco in 1873 and are still running there today. San Francisco is built on steep hills, making cable cars a very suitable form of transportation.

Electric power

Electricity was obviously the best source of power for streetcars. At first, it was difficult to devise a method that worked. Batteries attached to the car were not good as they made the car too heavy.

Then the electric generator was invented, making it possible to supply electricity from a central powerhouse. In 1886, a streetcar service opened in Montgomery, Alabama. The electricity was

◀ This is a trolleybus in Riga, Latvia, which is one of the many cities that still uses streetcars.

▲ *This modern tram operates in Croydon, England. Trams are making a comeback as cities search for ways of moving large numbers of people quickly, efficiently, and in an environmentally friendly way.*

generated from a powerhouse and traveled along an overhead wire. A small carriage ran along on top of the wire. A cable from this carriage was attached to the streetcar so that the electricity could reach it. The wheels of the car and the rails completed the electric circuit.

The real breakthrough came in 1888 when Frank J. Sprague invented the swivel trolley pole. This pole connected the streetcar to the wire. The streetcar ran underneath the wire. Once this method came into use, streetcars spread all over the United States and the world. By 1902, there were nearly 22,000 miles (35,000 kilometers) of electrified railroads in the United States alone.

Trolleybuses

The main disadvantage of the streetcar was that it could not move away from its rails. This made changing streetcar routes difficult and expensive. Getting on and off could also be awkward—the

▶ *This illustration shows two designs for how a streetcar is connected to the overhead electrical current that provides power.*

streetcar could not pull into the curb, and people getting on and off had to walk into the street. Bus stops were often isolated in the middle of streets.

So experiments were made with trolleybuses that ran on wheels rather than rails and were also called trackless trolleys. However, they still depended on overhead wires for their power, so they were not really much better than streetcars. There are very few trolleybuses used around the world today.

trolleybus

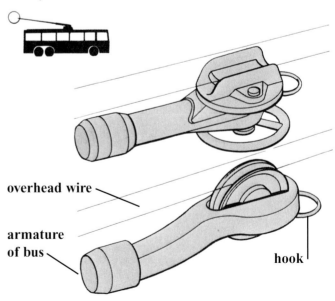

overhead wire

armature of bus

hook

DID YOU KNOW?

The word *bus* is short for the Latin word *omnibus*, meaning "for all"—in other words, a form of transportation for everyone to use, whether on land, sea, or in the air.

Modern buses

Until the 1920s, gasoline-powered buses were built from a truck chassis with a bus body on top. Then manufacturers started making vehicles with a chassis designed for a bus. The engine drove a generator, which powered electric motors that turned the wheels. In the late 1930s, the diesel engine began to take over from gasoline, because it was simpler, more robust, and cheaper to run.

Buses steadily increased in popularity because they did not suffer from the limitations of streetcars. They could change route easily, they did not require an expensive electrical supply system, and they did not need rails in the road. Today, there are small buses for short town and city routes with a lot of stops; school buses; bigger buses for long-distance intercity routes; and coaches for touring. Long-distance buses and tour coaches have compartments for storing luggage.

Articulated buses, or "bendy buses," entered service in Europe in the 1950s, and they are still used today. A bendy bus is essentially a bus towing a trailer. The two parts are connected by a flexible material and a continuous floor so that people can walk from one to the other. The bendy bus not only carries more people than a standard single-deck bus, but it is also more fuel efficient.

Another way to carry more people is to add a second passenger deck on top of the first. Double-decker buses are popular in busy towns and cities because they carry roughly twice as many people without taking up any more space on the road.

▶ *Two cable cars cross on Hyde Street, San Francisco. The city's cable car system began operation in 1873. Today, the system operates 40 cars on three lines that extend nearly 5 miles (8 kilometers) through the hilliest parts of San Francisco.*

▲ *Articulated, or bendy, buses are one way of carrying more people in a longer vehicle that is able to negotiate tight corners in busy city streets.*

Buses were traditionally operated by a driver and a conductor. The driver drove the vehicle while the conductor collected fares from customers. To reduce operating costs, modern buses are mainly operated by one person. The driver is responsible for collecting fares, or the bus may have an automatic entry system based on coins or tokens.

Alternative fuels

Each bus replaces many individual car journeys, so using buses reduces air pollution. However, diesel buses do produce air pollution. Diesel engines give out high levels of soot and chemicals such as nitrogen oxides (NO_x). Transportation companies in North America, Europe, and Japan are now experimenting with buses powered by cleaner fuels.

Experimental buses have been powered by hydrogen, natural gas, gasohol (a mixture of ethanol and gasoline), and fuel cells, which are devices that produce electricity by reacting hydrogen with oxygen.

Modern streetcars

Despite their disadvantages, streetcars are still used in many cities in the world because electric power is clean and quiet. The modern streetcar, or tram, is faster and quieter than the old type. Many still use swivel trolley poles linked to overhead wires. The pole is connected to the wire either by small wheels or by a mechanical device called a pantograph. This device is held against the wire by springs.

There is another kind of powering system, which is based on the cable car. Instead of moving cables, the slots in the street contain rails. These rails carry electricity from the power source. An attachment called a plow connects the streetcar to the rail.

There are not as many streetcars as there used to be. As world fuel supplies begin to run out, the electric streetcar might make a comeback. It is a good solution to the problems of traffic congestion and air pollution in cities. Some cities are considering excluding cars from their centers and using only streetcars and buses for transportation.

See also: CABLE TRAVEL • RAILROAD SYSTEM

Sublimation

If a large block of ice is placed in a freezer, it will slowly shrink until it disappears altogether. At the same time, ice will appear on the freezer pipes. The water in the ice block will have turned into water vapor by a process called sublimation.

Sublimation is not like heating a block of ice until it melts into water and then boils away as water vapor. The ice block in the freezer cannot turn into water because the temperature is below the melting point of ice. It turns into water vapor directly from solid ice. Snow, too, gradually disappears, even though the temperature stays well below freezing. Frost and snow form when water changes directly from a gas to the solid state. A solid substance will change into a vapor—without first becoming a liquid—when it is kept below its freezing point. Of course the freezing point of a substance varies with pressure. The greater the pressure, the higher the temperature at which the substance freezes.

Freeze-dried food

Food will keep for a long time when it is freeze-dried in a vacuum. The food is put in a chamber, most of the air is pumped out, and the chamber is cooled to below the freezing point of water. The frozen moisture in the food then becomes a vapor that is pumped out of the chamber. Sometimes the vapor may condense, as it does on the pipes in the freezer, and is removed as ice.

This way of removing the liquid from a substance has other uses, too. It is used to prepare the skins of animals to be stuffed in a process called taxidermy. As the water in the skin does not change to a liquid before it evaporates, the skin does not shrivel up and retains its original shape.

Dry ice

Many horror films have a scene with mist swirling around an old castle. This effect is usually achieved using solid frozen carbon dioxide (CO_2), called dry

▼ *The mist in this photograph of a pop concert is water vapor that has condensed out of warm moist air when it comes into contact with dry ice. Mist adds a feeling of suspense to films and theater productions.*

When solid iodine is heated in a test tube, violet iodine vapor sublimes and condenses again as black crystals.

ice. At ordinary atmospheric pressure, CO_2 will not form a liquid, hence the term *dry ice* for the solid form of the gas. The white mist is not the CO_2 gas, which is invisible. It is water vapor condensing out of the warm moist air when it touches the cold CO_2 gas and the even colder dry ice, just as the steam from a kettle condenses in the cooler air outside.

Iodine

Some substances can be isolated or purified by means of sublimation. Iodine is a bluish-black solid that sublimes. If iodine is mixed with another substance, it can be purified by heating the mixture until the iodine sublimes. The iodine changes directly to a violet-blue vapor. If a cool surface is placed nearby, vapor touching this surface condenses into a solid crust of pure iodine. Arsenic sublimes in a similar fashion. Substances that do not sublime at normal atmospheric pressure will sometimes sublime at lower pressures.

Sublimation printing

Most printers work by applying liquid ink or solid particles of toner to the surface of a sheet of paper. Dye sublimation printers use sublimation to produce high-quality printing. A print head heats solid dyes embedded in plastic. The heat vaporizes the dyes, which then permeate the paper before changing directly back into the solid state. Since the dyes are diffused throughout the paper instead of sitting on its surface, images printed in this way are less likely to fade or distort over time.

A comet's tail

Comets are small, icy bodies orbiting the Sun, usually on an elliptical (oval) path. When comets approach the Sun, they develop long bright tails. The tails consist of gases and particles of dust given off by the comet as the Sun constantly warms its frozen surface.

In the vacuum of space, water in the comet's surface cannot exist as a liquid. It changes directly from ice to the gaseous state. As it evaporates, particles of dust embedded in the ice are released from the comet's surface, and they fly away into space. Sunlight reflecting off these dust particles makes them visible to people, millions of miles away on Earth, as the comet's tail.

See *also:* ASTEROID, COMET, AND METEOR • FOOD TECHNOLOGY • PRINTING

Submarine

For centuries, people dreamed of traveling underwater in a boat, but it was only twentieth-century science and technology that made it possible to build a practical submarine. Now much of the activities of the world's navies takes place below the surface of the oceans in powerful submarines.

A practical submarine needs a steel body and an efficient engine that produces no harmful exhaust gases. In the late eighteenth century, engineers had the technology to build the hull, but there was no suitable power source available until the large electric motor driven by a number of storage batteries was developed in the late 1800s.

The ancient Greeks were the first to try designing an underwater craft, although it was probably never built. If it was, it is likely to have drowned its crew.

Italian artist, engineer, and scientist Leonardo da Vinci (1452–1519) left drawings for a submarine, and the Englishman William Bourne (1527–1591) designed one in 1578.

The earliest submarines

The first submarine that is known to have been built was shown to King James I (1566–1625) in the Thames River in London, England, in the 1620s. It was designed and built by the Dutch engineer Cornelis van Drebbel (1572–1633), who "sailed" the vessel down the river just under the surface.

A submarine built in the United States attacked British warships during the American War of Independence (1775–1783) in 1776. It had a drill worked from inside for boring into the wooden bottom of an enemy ship, so that a box of explosives could be attached. It was designed and built by U.S. inventor David Bushnell (1742–1824) and was called *Turtle*. Another submarine, called *Nautilus*, was successfully built by U.S. engineer and inventor Robert Fulton (1765–1815) in 1800 in France. The French tried various designs with some success, and in 1863 built *Plongeur* (Diver).

The first successful attack on a warship by a submarine was carried out in 1864, during the American Civil War (1861–1865), by the Confederate submarine *Hunley*. It sank the Federal ship USS *Housatonic*, but *Hunley* also sank itself.

Between the time of the American Civil War and the end of the nineteenth century, the main features of a modern submarine were gradually built into new boats. The first modern submarine to enter service with the U.S. Navy was the USS *Holland*, built by U.S. engineer John P. Holland (1840–1914) in 1900. The submarine finally proved its value in the successful German U-boat attacks on Allied shipping during in World War I (1914–1918).

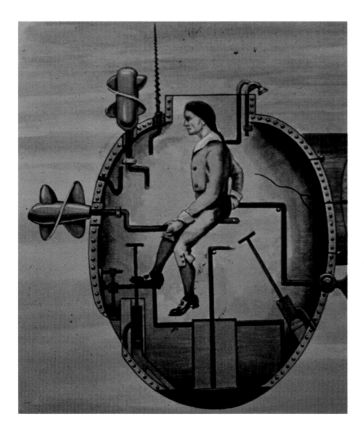

◀ *Turtle was a submarine built by David Bushnell in 1776. It was driven by two propellers worked by hand and carried a watertight box of explosives that could be attached to an enemy ship's hull with a drill.*

▶ *All the major navies used submarines during both world wars. During World War II, these German U-boats were particularly effective in attacking shipping bringing essential supplies across the Atlantic Ocean from the United States to Britain.*

How a submarine works

For thousands of years, people had used diving bells—large, heavy bell-shaped objects lowered into the water in which a diver could breathe the air trapped inside. They were useful for laying the foundations of bridges across rivers and for salvaging valuable cargoes from the wrecks of sunken ships resting on the seabed.

The first submarines were all designed as mobile diving bells. A diving bell sinks when lowered into the water because the bell is heavier than the amount of water it displaces. It is pulled to the surface again with a rope or chain. A submarine must sink and surface again on its own.

Letting water into compartments in the boat made it heavy enough to sink. But emptying it out again was the problem. Cornelius van Drebbel attached leather bags to his submarine and squeezed them flat to get the water out. In this way, he could sink and surface as often as he liked.

Later, hand pumps were used to empty the tanks of water. It was hard work, but it did the job eventually. It was not until the French submarine *Plongeur* was built in 1863 that compressed air was used to push the water out of the ballast tanks. It was fast and efficient, and it is the method still used today. The French took their compressed air down in large bottles. Today, the compressed air tanks are refilled by a motor compressor.

A submarine's engines

The earliest submarines were powered by oars, which was an inefficient way of traveling underwater. A more common way was for one or more crew members to turn propellers by hand. Even in the middle of the nineteenth century, this was the only way to move a submarine.

The only engines available were steam engines. These engines were more efficient, but they needed a great deal of air to burn the fuel and produced a

great deal of poisonous fumes in return. Then *Plongeur* demonstrated that it was possible to use a motor running on the same compressed air that controlled the buoyancy (the ability to float). This method worked, but it soon used up the compressed air that had been taken down when the submarine went underwater.

The answer came when storage batteries driving an electric motor were used. The batteries did not last very long, but they could be recharged over and over again by a second motor driving a generator. This could be a steam, gasoline, or diesel engine. These could be used only on the surface, where there was plenty of fresh air and where the poisonous exhaust fumes could be pushed out of the submarine. This second motor could also drive the submarine on the surface.

Therefore the modern submarine propulsion system was born. An air-breathing engine drove it on the surface and recharged the batteries at the same time. It also provided power to refill the compressed air tanks. Underwater, an electric motor turned the propeller.

Later, after World War II (1939–1945), nuclear-powered engines were made to drive submarines. These engines need no air, so they can be used when the submarine is submerged as well as when it is on the surface.

Steering

A modern submarine is steered by moving control surfaces. Rudders make it turn, and hydroplanes make it point up or down. It "flies" through the water in the same way as an airplane does in the air.

To submerge, a submarine fills its ballast tanks to overcome its buoyancy and points its front end down with the hydroplanes. When it reaches the right depth, it levels off with the hydroplanes and adjusts its depth by adding water or air to trim tanks until its buoyancy is neutral (neither too light nor too heavy). The trim tanks are also used to keep the boat level. If the front end is too light, the forward tanks are flooded.

Breathing underwater

In a diving bell, the divers often breathed just the air that had been trapped in the bell when it went down. This air supply did not last very long nor stay fresh. Later, a crude pump pushed air down a tube to the divers. A disadvantage was that if the pump stopped, the water pressure would push any air in the bell back up the tube. The pump had to be running all the time to maintain the air pressure and hold back the water in the bell.

When diesel engines were put in submarines to drive them on the surface and to recharge the batteries, it was not always safe for a boat to surface. So breathing tubes, called snorkels, were used. They were quite short, but they allowed the boat to stay under the surface while running its diesel engine. Fresh air was taken in through one tube, and the exhaust fumes expelled through another. In this way, submarines could stay underwater for much longer than before.

Modern submarines have equipment to clean and freshen the air so that the crew can breathe comfortably even when submerged for a long time.

The hull

Diving bells were made of metal. Small ones were made in one piece, cast in a mold. Large ones were made of several plates joined together. The first submarines were constructed from wood, and they were prone to leaking. Wood is flexible, and the cracks between the timbers had to be stuffed with fibers and pitch (a black, sticky substance) to keep the water out. It was not until the middle of the nineteenth century that the first submarine was made of cast iron.

▶ *On the surface (1), a submarine's tanks are nearly full of air. When it dives (2), the main vents (valves) open to let the air out. This also lets the water in through the free flood holes. When the tanks are full of water (or when the submarine has reached the right depth), the main vents are closed (3). To surface, compressed air is blown into the tanks, forcing water out through the free flood holes (4). At the surface, the rest of the water is forced out with fresh air (5) until the tanks are empty again (6).*

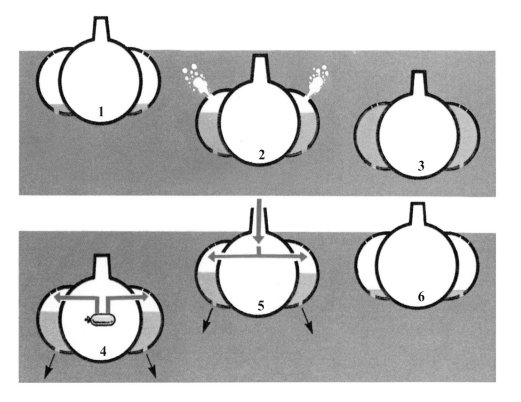

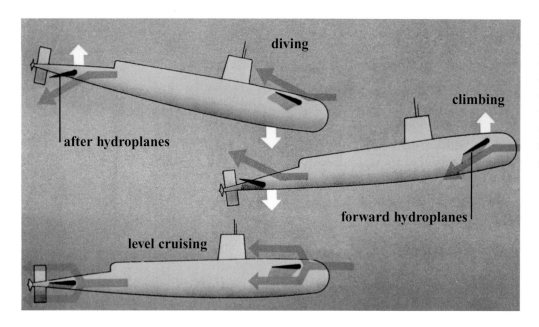

diving

after hydroplanes

climbing

forward hydroplanes

level cruising

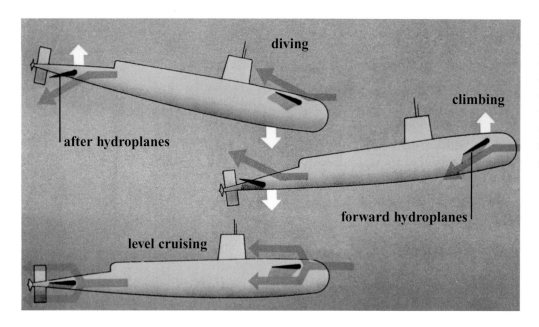 *A submarine "flies" through the water like an airplane in the air. It has hydroplanes similar to the elevators on a plane—two forward and two aft—to steer it up or down. It also has one or more rudders in its tail.*

How deep a submarine can descend depends on the strength of its hull. Steel plate is ideal for making a strong, watertight hull. The cross section of a modern submarine is as nearly circular as possible to give the greatest strength.

Part of the difficulty in making a really strong hull is that so many holes must be cut in it. There must be a hatchway for the crew to get in and out. The propeller, rudder, and hydroplane shafts must penetrate the hull. There must be holes for periscopes and snorkel tubes. All these holes weaken the hull. They all need to be tightly closed when the boat is submerged. Any weakness around a hole or in the mechanism for sealing it will reduce the maximum depth to which a submarine can descend. If there is any weakness, the submarine collapses under water pressure.

Weapons

Nearly all the submarines ever built have been ships of war, designed to attack enemy vessels. The first weapons they carried were usually some sort of explosive that could be attached to an enemy ship by drilling into its wooden hull. A long fuse gave the submarine time to escape before the explosion. Since the submarines were driven by hand, they could not catch a moving sailing ship. So they had to attack ships at anchor.

It was only in World War II that such methods were used successfully. The Italians, and later the British, made attacks on warships at anchor in harbors. They used two-person or four-person submarines to plant explosives on the hulls of enemy ships. The submarines were tiny, and the crew sat astride them wearing underwater breathing apparatus.

▶ *This is a medium-sized attack submarine, the USS Virginia. The smallest modern submarines displace up to about 9,000 tons (8,100 tonnes) when submerged and have a crew of up to 60 people. The largest submarines displace more than 25,000 tons (22,500 tonnes) submerged and carry a crew of 175 people.*

◄ *The control room of a modern submarine is crammed with electronic systems and displays for steering the submarine and detecting and attacking enemy vessels.*

▼ *Midget submarines were used to attack ships in harbor during World War II. Today, midget subs are mainly used to land special forces secretly in enemy territory.*

Torpedoes

Much more promising was an explosive device that would take itself to the target. This device was the motorized torpedo, first used successfully by English engineer Robert Whitehead (1823–1905) in the 1870s. The first torpedoes were attached to the outside of the submarine and released in range of the target. Later, they were pushed out of torpedo tubes in the hull. Once a method had been devised to close the seaward end of the tubes after the torpedoes had been fired, the tubes could be reloaded without the risk of flooding.

Modern torpedoes are very complicated pieces of machinery. They have computers to guide them and various kinds of devices for seeking out enemy ships and locking onto them from a distance.

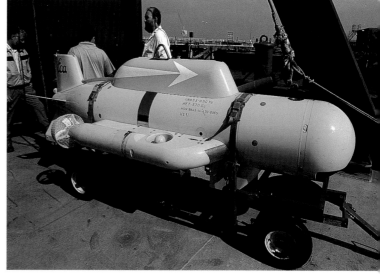

Guns

Up to World War II, submarines also carried a gun on the foredeck for combat on the surface. It was really only of use against an unarmed ship. Modern submarines no longer have guns on the foredeck, since submarines do not engage in combat on the surface. A submarine on the surface is highly vulnerable to attack. It can be detected readily by radar and can be destroyed by a missile from a ship or an airplane many miles away.

Missiles

The latest weapons are ballistic missiles. These rocket-powered weapons, which may carry nuclear warheads, are stored in tubes pointing upward. Hatches on the deck cover the tubes. The missiles

can be fired when the submarine is submerged many feet below the surface and have a range of 7,500 miles (12,000 kilometers).

Navigation underwater

Early submarines had to come to the surface to find out where they were. Then a periscope was installed to let the captain see all around the boat without breaking the surface of the water.

Navigating a submarine underwater over a distance was a very difficult task that depended as much on luck as on science. Now, a submarine navigator relies on a submarine inertial navigation system (SINS). This very sensitive device detects any movement of the boat in any direction. If the starting position of the boat is fed into the system, SINS can plot the boat's position at any time after that. Every few days, the boat's position can be checked by other means, such as radar, radio beacons, satellites, and even sextants.

Nuclear-powered craft

It is the coming of the nuclear-powered submarine that has made SINS so vital. A nuclear submarine can stay submerged for months at a time. It needs no fresh air or fresh water. It can go for years without having to refuel. It can send and receive radio messages and even radar by sending an antenna up to the surface.

But radio and radar signals can be detected by an enemy, who will be able to pinpoint the position of the submarine. So, to be absolutely safe, a submarine must make no contact with the surface at all, even for navigation.

◀ *Missile submarines launch their missiles without breaking the surface of the water. Trident II missiles currently used by U.S. Navy submarines are 46 feet (14 meters) long and carry up to 12 independent warheads. Each missile can attack up to 12 different targets in different places.*

See also: ARCHIMEDES • DIVING • GYROSCOPE • MISSILE AND TORPEDO • PROPELLER • SONAR • SUBMERSIBLE • WARSHIP

Submersible

A submersible is a small submarine used for peaceful purposes only. Submersibles can take divers down to work safely underwater. Submersibles also take scientists and explorers deep underwater to study the life and geology that exist there.

The word *submersible* means any craft that can submerge, or go under the water. Diving bells were the first submersibles. These were cylinders or bell-shaped chambers, open at the bottom. When diving bells were lowered into the water, a person inside could breathe the air inside until the oxygen was used up. Later, hand pumps were used to pump more air down to submerged diving bells.

▼ *This submersible is being lowered into the sea from its mother ship to begin its descent into the deep.*

The bathysphere

From 1930 to 1934, U.S. marine zoologist Charles William Beebe (1877–1962) and engineer Otis Barton (born 1899) carried out a series of dives in the Caribbean Sea in an underwater vessel they had built. They called their vessel a bathysphere, from the Greek words *bathys,* meaning "deep," and *sphere,* meaning "rounded shape." Beebe's and Barton's dives included a record-breaking one of 3,028 feet (923 meters). They became the first people to see the completely black underwater world below 1,000 feet (300 meters).

The bathysphere was made of steel and was only 5 feet (1.5 meters) in diameter. It was shaped like a ball—the best design for withstanding the tremendous pressure of the surrounding water. The vessel contained oxygen cylinders that the men used to control their breathing supply. It also had three tiny portholes made from thick quartz. The bathysphere had to be lowered on a steel cable from a ship on the surface. There was a telephone link,

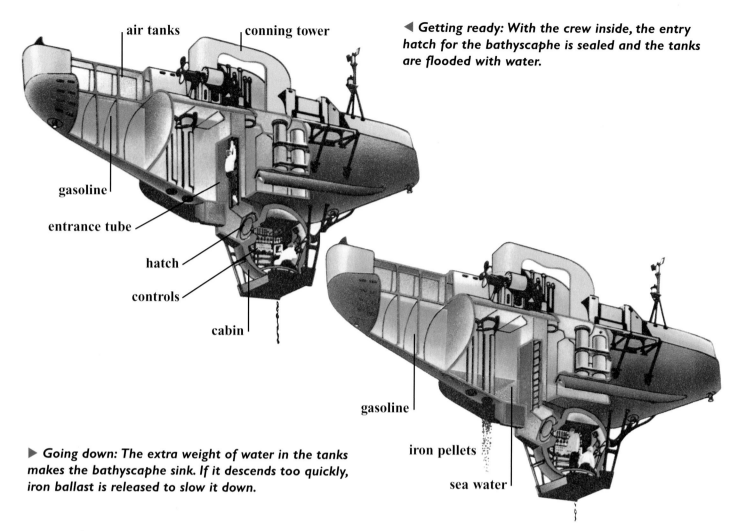

air tanks

conning tower

gasoline

entrance tube

hatch

controls

cabin

◄ Getting ready: With the crew inside, the entry hatch for the bathyscaphe is sealed and the tanks are flooded with water.

gasoline

iron pellets

sea water

▶ Going down: The extra weight of water in the tanks makes the bathyscaphe sink. If it descends too quickly, iron ballast is released to slow it down.

too, so that Beebe and Barton could keep in touch with the surface. Yet the bathysphere had several disadvantages. Because of the cable link, it could not move around, and it could not go as deep as the scientists would have liked. In rough seas, there were dangerous stresses in the supporting cable.

The bathyscaphe

A few years after Beebe and Barton's work, Swiss physicist and high-altitude balloonist Auguste Piccard (1884–1962) designed the bathyscaphe. This name came from the Greek words *bathys,* meaning "deep," and *scaphos,* meaning "ship." The bathyscaphe was simply a crew sphere, just like the bathysphere, hanging from a massive float. However, the bathyscaphe could go even deeper and did not need to be tied to a ship on the surface. It was driven by two small screw propellers, worked by battery-powered motors.

The bathyscaphe was a high-quality steel sphere with an inside diameter of 6½ feet (2 meters). The steel walls were 3½ inches (9 centimeters) thick, strengthened to 6 inches (15 centimeters) around the portholes and door. The portholes had to be tremendously strong and perfectly sealed to the surrounding metal. The transparent, plexiglass windows were constructed like cones with their narrow ends sliced off. These cones were then placed, narrow end inward, into a matching hole in the steel hull. As the pressure of water increased during the dive, it pushed the port windows more securely into the hole in the hull.

Operating the bathyscaphe

The top part of the bathyscaphe was a large metal float, shaped like a ship's hull. This float was divided into compartments, some filled with gasoline, others with air. As gasoline is lighter than

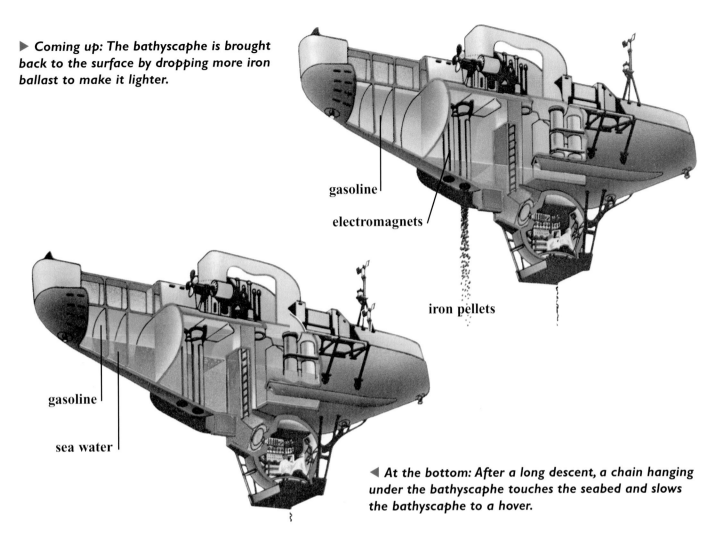

▶ **Coming up: The bathyscaphe is brought back to the surface by dropping more iron ballast to make it lighter.**

gasoline

electromagnets

iron pellets

gasoline

sea water

◀ **At the bottom: After a long descent, a chain hanging under the bathyscaphe touches the seabed and slows the bathyscaphe to a hover.**

water, it gave the craft buoyancy. Once the crew was aboard, the air tanks and the entrance tube were flooded with seawater, which made the bathyscaphe heavier, and it sank slowly beneath the waves. As the vessel continued its descent, seawater entered the gasoline tanks. This kept the pressure inside the float the same as the water pressure outside, preventing the outside pressure from crushing the float like a paper bag.

As the bathyscaphe went deeper, the seawater became colder and chilled the gas in the tanks. The cold made the gas contract, so more seawater entered the float. The bathyscaphe became heavier and heavier, and it began to dive faster. To slow the dive down, the crew released some iron pellets that were carried as ballast. Several tons of these tiny metal balls were stored in two special containers under the float. They were held in place by electromagnets, powerful magnets operated by

sending electric current through coils of wire. To release some iron pellets, the crew merely had to cut off the electric current for a few seconds, and pellets fell to the seabed. This system ensured that the crew had very accurate control over the ballast system. It also meant that if the electricity supply were accidentally cut off, the bathyscaphe would rise to the surface automatically.

Beneath the cabin of the bathyscaphe hung a length of heavy chain. When the vessel was nearing the seabed, the chain touched the bottom first. The vessel became lighter because some of the heavy chain was resting on the seabed. The bathyscaphe then hovered above the bottom and carried out its scientific research.

The steel sphere held two people with enough air for about 24 hours. In addition to the controls for raising and lowering the craft, there were mechanical arms and a probe to test whether the seabed was solid or not. Powerful lights were needed to pierce the total darkness of the undersea world. Cameras and sonar equipment were also carried to record scenes on the seabed and map the underwater landscape.

The history of the bathyscaphe

The bathyscaphe was first tested off the coast of West Africa in 1948. In a second version of the craft called the *Trieste*, Auguste Piccard went down to a depth of over 2 miles (3 kilometers). In 1958, the U.S. Navy took over the development of the bathyscaphe. The vessel was taken to California and a new cabin was fitted.

On January 23, 1960, Jacques Piccard, Auguste's son, and Lt. Donald Walsh of the U.S. Navy descended into the depths of the Marianas Trench in the Pacific Ocean. They reached a depth of 35,802 feet (10,912 meters), a world record. The pressure at this depth is 1,100 times greater than at the surface of the ocean.

Modern submersibles are designed to work at a particular maximum depth. Some are made for shallow seas only, such as the North Sea between Britain and Norway. They would not be of any use working on the bed of the Atlantic Ocean. Deep-sea submersibles have to be made much stronger.

What submersibles can do

Submersibles are made and equipped to carry out many different tasks underwater. Some are designed just to take people down to the bottom of the sea to find out what is there. These survey

▲ Remotely Operated Vehicles (ROVs), such as the one in this picture, have no crew onboard. Instead, they are operated from the mother ship. Powerful lights and TV cameras are fitted to the submersible before it is submerged so that the operator can see where the submersible is going.

◄ This picture shows the **Alvin** research submersible and its mother ship. This vessel helped to salvage a hydrogen bomb that was lost in 1966 and to explore the wreck of the passenger liner **Titanic**, which sank in 1912.

▶ *During a dive in a submersible, scientists spend most of their time peering out of the windows at the fish and other creatures that glide within range of the craft's lights.*

submersibles are equipped with strong lights and TV cameras so that the crew can see and record their environment. Surveys of the seabed are needed before any kind of work can be done there. If a cable is to be laid or a bridge built, it may be essential to have a detailed survey first.

Another simple use for a submersible is to take divers down from the mother ship to the seabed. There they leave the submersible through a system of watertight doors to work outside in the water. Usually a supervisor stays inside the submersible to observe the divers and their work. The supervisor can signal to the divers and also communicate with the mother ship if necessary.

A diver who becomes ill or is hurt in an accident can be quickly taken into the submersible for treatment. This way of working is called diver lockout, and the submersible must have special hatchways to let the divers in and out while underwater. A particular advantage of this system is that the divers' compartment can be pressurized to the same degree as the depth at which they are working. (The pilot's compartment is pressurized at normal atmospheric pressure.) The submersible can take divers up from deep water and transfer them to a decompression chamber in the mother ship. This lets the divers return to normal atmospheric pressure in the comfort of the mother ship without having to make a slow ascent from the deep. It saves time and also prevents the bends, the dangerous condition when bubbles of nitrogen form in the blood of divers who surface too quickly.

Rescue vessels

More complicated submersibles have mechanical arms with tools at the end for doing a wide variety of jobs. These tools are operated from inside the submersible. The crew may have a window, called a viewport, to look through and see the tool at work. Other submersibles have TV cameras, and the crew looks at a TV screen. The mechanical arms are worked by hydraulics. They may have several joints, so that they can be moved as precisely and delicately as a human hand.

Air in the submersible is recirculated, and the same air is breathed by the crew again and again. It is taken through a filter and purifier called a scrubber. The divers in a diver lockout craft have their own separate supply of breathing gas (generally a mixture of helium and oxygen) in their specially pressurized compartment.

One vital use for submersibles is to rescue people trapped in submarines or other submersibles that have failed to come to the surface after an accident or power failure. The trapped people may have an aqualung called SCUBA (self-contained underwater breathing apparatus) that they can use in an emergency. It may be possible to get them out of their craft and into the rescue submersible.

If the trapped divers cannot be released, rescuers may be able to raise the submersible itself, using cables and lifting gear. In this case, the rescue craft has the job of attaching the cables.

▲ *In this picture, the robotic arm of a submersible retrieves a leaded glass window from the wreck of the passenger liner* **Titanic**. *Crewed and uncrewed submersibles have explored the wreck.*

The tools

The tool on the end of a submersible's mechanical arm might be a device, like a steel claw, for grasping things. It can be used for moving heavy objects out of the way, or for taking back samples of rock from the seabed to the surface.

The arms can carry drilling and cutting tools for digging out samples or repairing underwater structures. Powerful pumps and tubes can be used to dig trenches for cables. The pump pushes a powerful jet of water through the tube, which the mechanical arm points in the right direction. This method is also useful for clearing mud and debris from a wreck or a structure that is to be repaired. Suction tubes can suck loose material from the seabed so that it can be examined on the surface. Welding and cutting with oxyacetylene torches is possible even underwater. The flame is so hot that the water cannot put it out.

Propulsion

All submersibles have motors powered by a large bank of electric storage batteries. The batteries also run the lighting, both for inside the submersible and for illuminating the scene outside. Power is needed for the hydraulics that work the various mechanical arms and tools.

The motors drive thruster propellers that push the submersible through the water and nudge it upward, downward, and to the left and right. These motors are used for getting the submersible into the right position and for holding it there against the current or tide.

Discovery of a legend

One of the best-known and busiest of submersibles is *Alvin,* an ocean-floor research vessel operated by Woods Hole Oceanographic Institute in Massachusetts. Perhaps its most dramatic dive was to "visit" the *Titanic*—a huge passenger liner that in 1912 sank in 12,500 feet (3,800 meters) of water after hitting an iceberg off the coast of Newfoundland. Though its exact location was unknown, the wreckage was finally found in 1985 by a robot craft called *Argo*. In 1986, it was seen directly for the first time by scientists who were carried down to it by the *Alvin*.

The *Alvin* was originally built of a combination of aluminum and fiberglass, with a steel sphere to hold the crew. Later, titanium replaced the aluminum and steel, walls were thickened, and the craft lengthened—all to allow diving to a depth of 13,120 feet (4,000 meters).

The mother ship

All submersibles must have people on the surface to help the crew and maintain the vessel. Even when diving close to shore, it is necessary to have a place nearby where the crew can eat and sleep between dives. The submersible needs regular servicing. So it must be lifted out of the water by a crane on the mother ship. When the submersible has finished a job in one place, it will be taken to its next job by the mother ship.

See also: DIVING • HYDRAULICS • OCEAN • PRESSURE • PROPELLER • REMOTE CONTROL • SONAR • SUBMARINE

Sulfur

Sulfur is a chemical element with the symbol S. It is not a metal and is one of the few elements to be found naturally in its pure form, as well as in combination with other elements. Sulfur has many uses and is a valuable mineral resource.

Sulfur has been known to humanity for many thousands of years. In prehistoric times, it was used as a pigment for cave painting. The Greek poet Homer (ninth to eighth century BCE) was one of the first to mention the medical use of sulfur. Sulfur in its natural state is found on the Mediterranean island of Sicily. As a result, its uses, such as for the bleaching of textiles, were familiar to the ancient Greeks and Romans. Sulfur is also called brimstone (from the German word *Brennstein*, which means "burning stone"), and the strange qualities of this substance fascinated alchemists and magicians during the Middle Ages.

It was not until the work of French chemist Antoine-Laurent Lavoisier (1743–1794) that sulfur was classified as a chemical element. Sulfur is now used in the heat treatment of rubber (in a process called vulcanization), in the manufacture of gunpowder and matches, and in medicine. Sulfur is also a good insulator against heat and electrical current.

Sulfur crystals

At room temperature, sulfur is normally a yellow crystalline solid. It has no taste or smell. It burns in air with a blue flame and a stifling odor. The crystals of sulfur occur in two distinct forms called allotropes. They are referred to by the first two letters of the Greek alphabet, *alpha* and *beta*.

Alpha sulfur is the more stable of the two allotropes. Its crystals are of a structure and shape known as an orthorhombic structure, and it melts at 235°F (113°C). But at high temperatures (above 203°F/95°C), beta sulfur is more stable. The crystals of beta sulfur are said to be monoclinic in structure, and this allotrope does not melt until it reaches a temperature of 246°F (119°C).

Changes from one state to another normally take place only over a period of time. If alpha sulfur is heated rapidly, it melts before any beta sulfur crystals are formed. In the same way, beta sulfur that is rapidly cooled will keep its monoclinic structure for a day or so before taking on the structure of alpha sulfur. Crystals of the alpha allotrope can be created directly if sulfur is dissolved in carbon disulfide (CS_2).

▶ *Sulfur consists of crystals, which can take one of two forms—orthorhombic or monoclinic.*

◄ *Sulfur is a main ingredient of gunpowder used in fireworks. Pure sulfur burns with a yellow flame.*

Flowers of sulfur can be prepared by sublimation (a process in which a solid is turned, by heating, into vapor, which returns to solid form on cooling). Flowers of sulfur consist of a fine powder that contains amorphous sulfur.

Mining for sulfur

Sulfur is found in large quantities in Japan, Russia, Europe, the United States, and Mexico. The traditional method of mining, long the practice in Sicily, is to burn the rock containing the sulfur in kilns with a limited supply of air. Part of the sulfur burns away, but part melts out as pure sulfur.

The large amount of sulfur to be found in the United States and Mexico is normally 200 yards (180 meters) underground, and it is difficult to reach. German-born U.S. scientist Hermann Frasch (1851–1914) invented a new way of mining this sulfur. A well is sunk into the rocks containing the sulfur. It consists of three tubes—an inner, a middle, and an outer tube. Water, superheated to 382°F (180°C), is passed down the outer tube under pressure, and compressed air is pumped down the inner tube. The water melts the sulfur, and the compressed air forces it up through the middle tube. It comes to the surface in a froth but is piped into vats where it solidifies. This sulfur is 99 percent pure and ready for industrial use.

Not all sulfur is mined. Natural gas contains hydrogen sulfide (H_2S), which can be processed to produce sulfur. Coal-fired power stations and the metal industry also provide sulfur from their waste gases: sulfur dioxide (SO_2) is a useful source. Compounds of sulfur have many uses in the laboratory, particularly sulfuric acid (H_2SO_4) and hydrogen sulfide, which is a poisonous gas that smells like rotten eggs.

Noncrystal forms

Sulfur does not always occur in a crystalline form. Plastic, or amorphous (shapeless), sulfur can be formed by pouring liquid sulfur that is almost boiling into cold water. After standing for a time, however, plastic sulfur becomes crystalline again. Amorphous sulfur can be formed by various methods, for example, by the action of light upon sulfur when it is dissolved in carbon disulfide.

See also: CRYSTAL • ELEMENT, CHEMICAL • INSULATOR • MINING AND QUARRYING • SUBLIMATION

Sun

The Sun is Earth's star. It is a huge ball of hot, glowing gases and is like many other stars in the universe. The Sun appears larger and brighter than the others because it is so much closer to Earth. Like other stars, the Sun is made up mainly of hydrogen and helium. The Sun gets its energy from nuclear reactions that take place deep within its core.

Of all the heavenly bodies, the Sun is by far the most important to people. Without the Sun's light and heat, Earth would be a dark, cold, and lifeless world. Many thousands of years ago, prehistoric peoples realized how important the Sun was and how its movements followed a pattern, and they worshiped it as a god. In more recent times, so did the Egyptians and the Aztec, Inca, and Maya civilizations of Central and South America. They built great pyramids and temples that were aligned with certain positions of the Sun in the sky.

The ancient Greek philosophers and astronomers were not as impressed. They considered the Sun to be just another heavenly body circling around Earth. Earth, not the Sun, was the center of the universe to the ancient Greeks.

In 1543, Polish astronomer Nicolaus Copernicus (1473–1543) put the astronomical record straight. He stated correctly that it is Earth that circles around the Sun. The Sun is the center and focal point of the solar system. Earth is a mere planet circling around it, along with eight other planets and many other smaller bodies.

How far away?

In order of distance from the Sun, Earth is the third planet, after Mercury and Venus. Earth lies, on average, about 93 million miles (150 million kilometers) away from the Sun. Astronomers call

▲ *Just before sunset, the Sun may take on a reddish glow. Earth's atmosphere scatters the blue and green colors in sunlight more than the longer wavelength orange and red colors. When the Sun is low in the sky, sunlight travels a greater distance through the atmosphere than when it is high in the sky, so the scattering effect is greater.*

this distance 1 astronomical unit (AU). It takes the Sun's light just over 8 minutes to travel to Earth. Another distance unit that astronomers use is the parsec, which is equal to about 3⅓ light-years.

The Sun is by far the largest body in the solar system. Its diameter is some 865,000 miles (1,392,000 kilometers), more than one hundred times the diameter of Earth. Even though it is made up of gas, the Sun is so big that it has a huge mass—more than 300,000 times the mass of Earth. This mass gives it a gravitational pull powerful enough to keep the planets circling in their orbits.

▶ *The Sun's warmth and light are essential for most of the life on Earth. The action of solar radiation on the skin produces some of the body's requirement for vitamin D as well as a suntan, but too much sunshine can be dangerous. Ultraviolet and infrared rays in sunshine can burn the skin and damage the genetic material in cells, leading to skin cancer. Too much sunbathing can also lead to premature aging of the skin.*

The Sun's motion

From Earth, the Sun is seen to rise in the east, arc across the sky, and set in the west. However, this is only an apparent motion, which happens because Earth is spinning in space on its axis from west to east. The Sun is seen to rise higher in the sky in summer than in winter. This occurs because Earth's spin-axis is tilted. As Earth circles in orbit around the Sun during the year, a particular place on the surface is tilted more toward the Sun at some times than at others. This brings about the seasons.

The greatest tilt occurs on about June 21 and December 21 every year. On June 21, the Northern Hemisphere is tilted most toward the Sun, and it is midsummer. On December 21, the Northern Hemisphere is tilted farthest away from the Sun, and it is midwinter. Around those two dates, the Sun rises to nearly the same height in the sky for several days. These dates are known as the solstices.

The daily and yearly "movements" of the Sun are therefore apparent motions caused by Earth's spin and its motion around the Sun. Most heavenly bodies move in this way, spinning on their axis as they orbit other celestial bodies. The Sun spins on its axis once every 25 Earth-days. It circles in a huge orbit in space around the center of the galaxy to

▼ *The McMath-Pierce solar telescope at the Kitt Peak National Observatory in Arizona has been used by astronomers to study the Sun since 1962.*

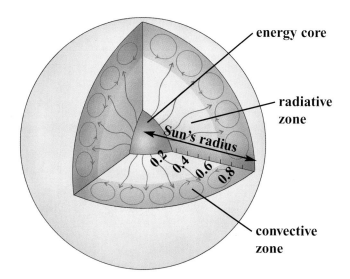

energy core

radiative zone

Sun's radius

0.2 0.4 0.6 0.8

convective zone

▲ *The fusion of hydrogen nuclei in the Sun's core releases energy that radiates outward through part of Sun called the radiative zone. Three-quarters of the distance from the core, a different process takes over. Energy is carried the rest of the way by rising columns of hot gas. This process is called convection, and it occurs in part of the Sun called the convective zone.*

which it belongs—the Milky Way galaxy. The Sun is one of some 100,000 million stars in the Milky Way. It is located about 30,000 light-years from the center of the Milky Way, and it orbits the center in about 225 million years.

The Sun is an average star. It is of average size and brightness and gives off a mainly yellowish light. Astronomers classify the Sun as a yellow dwarf.

Observing the Sun

The Sun is of special interest to astronomers because it is the only star that they can study closely and send space probes to investigate.

Astronomers use special telescopes to study the Sun. These solar telescopes usually take the form of tall towers that reflect and focus an image of the Sun onto a surface and into instruments that analyze the light. This method of projection is the only safe way for anyone to observe the Sun. Looking at the Sun directly through a telescope or pair of binoculars may cause blindness. Looking at the Sun with the naked eye and even through a piece of smoked or tinted glass is also unsafe.

The world's largest solar telescope—the McMath-Pierce—is located at the Kitt Peak National Observatory in Arizona. Its heliostat (light-gathering mirror) is 80 inches (2.1 meters) across and mounted atop a 100-foot- (30-meter-) tall tower. It reflects sunlight 500 feet (150 meters) down a long inclined shaft. A 60-inch (1.5-meter) mirror reflects the sunlight back to ground level to another mirror, which projects a 30-inch- (76-centimeter-) wide image of the Sun onto an observing table.

Over the past few decades, the Sun has also been observed from space satellites. Satellites are valuable because they can study the Sun not only in ordinary visible light, but also at other wavelengths. The Sun radiates energy at all wavelengths—from short gamma rays to long radio waves. Earth's atmosphere blocks most of these wavelengths, but satellites orbit above the atmosphere and can therefore record the Sun at all wavelengths.

Extensive space observations of the Sun were made in the 1970s by U.S. astronauts in the space station *Skylab*. More recently, a series of satellites and space probes, including the Solar and Heliospheric Observatory (SOHO), *Ulysses*, and Cluster missions have studied the Sun from space.

The Sun's surface

The visible surface of the Sun, which radiates light, is called the photosphere. Its average temperature is about 10,000°F (5500°C). Energy from the Sun's core (center) is carried outward by columns of gas that make the Sun's surface look grainy, an effect called granulation. The graininess can be seen with standard optics.

DID YOU KNOW?

The Solar and Heliospheric Observatory (SOHO) was launched in 1995 to study the Sun. Its mission was originally intended to last two years, but it has been extended twice so that it could observe the Sun over a complete 11-year solar cycle.

▶ *Prominences and flares send vast fountains of gas exploding out of the Sun's stormy surface into space.*

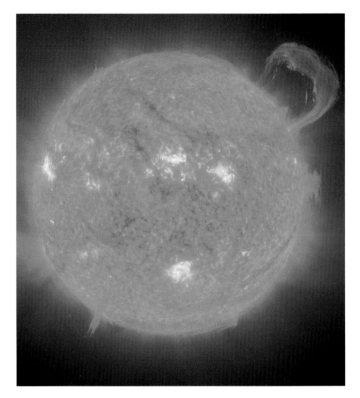

From time to time, a number of dark patches, called sunspots, appear on the surface of the Sun. The central part of a spot is the darkest and is called the umbra. The umbra is surrounded by a lighter region called the penumbra.

Sunspots are somewhat cooler than the rest of the Sun's surface—about 7000°F (4000°C). They may grow up to 10,000 miles (16,000 kilometers) across. On average, sunspots last for a week or so, but some may remain visible for several months.

The amount of sunspot activity varies widely from year to year. There are times when the Sun has few, if any, spots. There are also times when it is covered with as many as one hundred spots. It has been found that the number of sunspots varies in a regular way over 11 years. This period is called the sunspot cycle. There was a sunspot maximum in 2000, so the next one will probably be in 2011.

The Sun has overall a weak magnetic field, but in the region of a sunspot the field becomes intense—about 2,500 times stronger than Earth's. This often causes sudden outbursts of brilliant light from the sunspot, a phenomenon called a flare. The flare

▼ *The Sun shines as a result of the same nuclear fusion reactions that make a hydrogen bomb explode.*

gives rise to streams of high-energy atomic particles, which shoot off into space. When they reach Earth, the particles disturb the upper atmosphere. This disrupts long-distance radio communications and power grids and sets off brilliant displays called auroras (radiant-colored lights) in the polar regions. These disturbances increase during periods of raised solar activity when the sunspot cycle is near its maximum.

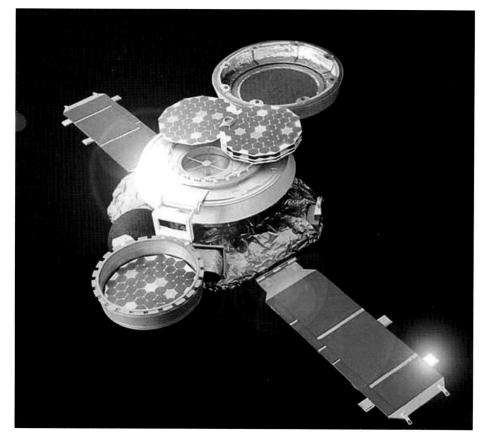

▶ *The* **Genesis** *space probe returned to Earth in 2004 after a three-year mission to collect particles from the Sun. However, its parachute landing system failed and it plowed into the Utah desert, destroying much of the probe's equipment.*

As well as these violent outbursts of high-energy particles, the Sun emits a stream of low-energy particles all the time, called the solar wind.

The Sun's atmosphere

Above the surface of the Sun are layers of gases that make up the Sun's outer atmosphere. The layer closest to the surface is called the chromosphere because of its pink-red color. Normally the chromosphere cannot be seen because it is masked by the intense light of the photosphere. Only when the photosphere is blotted out can the chromosphere be seen.

> ### DID YOU KNOW?
>
> The Sun's mass makes up 99.8 percent of the total mass of the solar system. At its center, the temperature of the Sun is about 27 million degrees Fahrenheit (15 million degrees Celsius).

The chromosphere can be seen only during a total eclipse of the Sun. A total eclipse occurs when the Moon comes directly between the Sun and Earth. It is a coincidence that the disk of the Moon is almost exactly the same size as the disk of the Sun when viewed from Earth. So during a total eclipse the Moon blots out the Sun's glaring photosphere and the fainter chromosphere becomes visible.

Rising up through the chromosphere are jets of hot gas, called spicules, which look like flames. They reach a height of up to 10,000 miles (16,000 kilometers). In places, enormous fountains of gas, called prominences, shoot out from the chromosphere. They may reach heights of several hundred thousand miles above the Sun's surface. They travel in great loops, or arcs, following the direction of the Sun's magnetic field.

The outermost layer of the Sun's atmosphere is called the corona. It extends from the denser chromosphere millions of miles out into space. It is difficult to say where it ends—it gradually becomes much thinner, just as the Earth's atmosphere does.

◀ *When sunlight is spread out into a spectrum, it is crossed by some 25,000 dark lines. These lines are produced by atoms in the Sun's atmosphere absorbing the sunlight at certain wavelengths as it streams out from the interior. The lines reveal the chemical elements contained within the Sun.*

The corona can be seen in nature only during a total solar eclipse, but it can be studied at other times using an instrument called a coronagraph. This creates an artificial eclipse. The corona is visible as a pearly white halo. Its temperature is as high as 3.6 million degrees Fahrenheit (2 million degrees Celsius).

Makeup of the Sun

The Sun consists mainly of hydrogen and helium, which are the two most plentiful elements in the universe. It also contains smaller quantities of nearly 70 other elements as well. The elements have been identified by studying sunlight in a special instrument called a spectroscope.

When sunlight is passed through a spectroscope, it spreads out into a spectrum, or rainbow, of colors. The Sun's spectrum is broken up by many dark lines. These are often called the Fraunhofer lines, named for German physicist Josef Fraunhofer (1787–1826). Each element produces a unique set of spectral lines. The positions of these lines tell astronomers which elements are present in the Sun.

The nuclear furnace

The Sun has been shining for about 4.6 billion years, radiating an unbelievable amount of energy. Where does this energy come from? It cannot come from combustion; otherwise the Sun would have burned out after a few million years. A different process is at work, called nuclear fusion.

During nuclear fusion, the nuclei (centers) of light atoms fuse to form the nuclei of heavier atoms. This process will take place only at very high pressure and temperatures. When fusion of light nuclei takes place, a small amount of their mass is converted into energy according to Albert Einstein's famous mass-energy equation:

$$E = mc^2$$

At the Sun's center, the temperature is hot enough for fusion to occur. Nuclei of hydrogen atoms fuse to form the nuclei of helium atoms. Every second, the Sun converts 4 million tons (3.5 million tonnes) of matter into energy.

Astronomers think that the Sun has used about half of the hydrogen in its core. In five billion years, the core hydrogen will be used up. The core will collapse, becoming warm enough to fuse helium into carbon and oxygen. Hydrogen fusion will also begin to occur in the outer layers, which will expand to produce a red giant. Eventually, hydrogen and helium fusion will be complete and the Sun will contract to become a white dwarf, not much bigger than the Earth. As its energy radiates away, the white dwarf Sun will fade. It will disappear from view and merge with the inky blackness of space.

See also: ASTRONOMY • ECLIPSE • GRAVITY • MOON • SOLAR ENERGY • SOLAR SYSTEM • STAR

Superconductivity

Normal conducting wires do not conduct electricity perfectly. There is resistance to the flow of electrical current. At very cold temperatures this resistance disappears for some metals, and they become superconductors.

Materials have strange properties at the low temperatures near absolute zero (–459.67°F or –273.15°C). These supercold materials are produced by the science of cryogenics. At supercold temperatures one of the properties of some metals is that they have no electrical resistance.

Electrical resistance

Even good conductors of electricity, such as copper, have some resistance when an electrical current flows through them. Because of this resistance, a cable cannot carry more than a limited amount of electricity unless it is made thicker. The cables needed to carry large amounts of electrical energy are often very thick and therefore expensive.

Electrical resistance reduces steadily as temperature falls. Scientists thought that resistance in conductors would fall to nothing only at absolute zero temperature. But research and experimentation at supercold temperatures has shown that electrical resistance suddenly drops to almost nothing at a few degrees above absolute zero. If any material is cooled to below this temperature, it becomes superconducting.

A voltage must be applied to keep electricity flowing through a normal wire, such as from a battery. With a superconductor, no battery is

▼ *When a superconducting material is cooled by liquid nitrogen, a magnet placed above it floats in midair. The magnet makes an electrical current flow in the superconductor. The current creates a magnetic field, which repels the magnet and makes it float. This phenomenon is called the Meissner effect.*

▲ *Superconductors have been used in experimental magnetic levitation trains, or maglevs, such as this Transrapid monorail running on a test track in Lathen, Germany. Superconducting electromagnets produce magnetic fields so powerful that they can raise the train above a track that also has powerful magnets embedded in it. There is no friction in the system because there is no contact between the train and the track. As a result, very high speeds are possible.*

needed because the electrical resistance is zero. This effect can be seen if a coil of wire is cooled in liquid helium. If a voltage is applied, the coil becomes an electromagnet, deflecting a compass placed nearby. The compass shows that the electromagnet keeps working even when the voltage is taken away because the electrical current continues to flow through the superconducting coil.

Zero-point energy

In a normal conductor, the voltage drives electrons through the metal, producing an electrical current. Imperfections in the metal, such as impurities, cause resistance to the movement of the electrons. Vibrations of the atoms also scatter some of the electrons and increase the electrical resistance. At lower temperatures, the atomic vibrations slow down so that there is less scattering and lower electrical resistance.

The vibrational energy of atoms at absolute zero is the lowest possible and is called the zero-point energy. There is no extra energy available to scatter electrons and so they can pass through the metal unhindered. Scientists think that these electrons travel in weakly bound pairs, called Cooper pairs. The first electron pulls on the atoms it moves past. This distortion drags a second electron along behind the first. The second electron experiences less resistance. The overall effect is to let electrons pass through the metal more easily. This theory explains how the simplest materials—chemical elements—become superconductors, but scientists

DID YOU KNOW?

Superconductivity was first observed in 1911 in mercury by Dutch physicist Heike Kamerlingh Onnes (1853–1926).

do not yet fully understand how more complex molecules or compounds—combinations of elements—become superconductors.

Supermagnets

One use of superconductivity is to generate magnetic fields used in atomic research. Superconductors can carry large electrical currents, so a supercold electromagnet can produce huge magnetic fields. These magnets are used to accelerate atomic particles to near the speed of light in machines called cyclotrons and synchrotrons.

The magnet coils are cooled using supercold liquid helium. Care is taken not to let the current grow too large. If the magnet goes over a certain critical field strength, there is a danger of losing superconductivity. The heating effect of a large current without superconductivity could easily melt the coil.

The first superconducting electromagnets and wire were made in the 1960s using wire made from an alloy of niobium and titanium. The first superconducting particle accelerator was built in the United States in 1987. A new, second-generation superconducting wire will carry one hundred times the current of a copper wire of the same thickness and yet cost no more than a copper wire to manufacture. The wire is produced by "growing" a thin film of superconducting material on a flexible material. The technique was developed using experience gained from experiments carried out in space shuttle missions.

Electricity supplies

Normally electricity is sent through cables at very high voltages and low currents to help prevent the heat loss that occurs with large currents. Even so, 6 to 7 percent of the electricity generated in the United States is lost, due in part to the resistance of the cables. Superconductors may make it possible to send large amounts of electrical energy at low voltages and very high currents.

Superconducting cables would not need to be large because there would be no heating. But they would have to be kept permanently below the

critical temperature that transforms them into superconductors for their entire length. This process is difficult and costly.

Superconductors can also be used to store electricity, which conventionally is difficult. Large electrical currents flow around a ring endlessly if it is kept superconducting. In this way, underground coil systems could act as electrical reservoirs to store spare electricity until it is needed.

Cutting the cost

The liquid helium needed to cool materials to the point at which they lose electrical resistance is very expensive, making the superconductors expensive as well. In the late 1980s, new materials were discovered that overcome electrical resistance at temperatures above the boiling point of liquid nitrogen (–329°F or –196°C). Liquid nitrogen is much cheaper and easier to handle, creating less expensive superconductors.

Mercury becomes a superconductor at 4K (–452°F or –269°C). As scientists tested more materials, they discovered some that become superconductors at higher temperatures. Some materials are known to become superconductors at temperatures near 135K (–216°F or –138°C).

Superconductor types

Two different types of superconductors have been discovered. They are called Type I and Type II. Type I superconductors were the first to be discovered. They need the lowest temperatures to become superconductors, and they switch suddenly to a superconducting state when they reach the appropriate temperature. They are mainly metals such as lead, zinc, mercury, and tin. Type I superconductors are commonly known by scientists as soft superconductors.

▶ *The world's fastest computers, such as the Cray 2 supercomputer pictured here, generate a lot of heat because of their superfast electrical activity concentrated in such a small space. One way to minimize this heating effect is to use superconducting circuits. Parts of the computer are chilled in liquid helium or liquid nitrogen so that they become superconducting. Electrical resistance in these circuits disappears and therefore so does the heating effect.*

Type II superconductors are mainly metallic compounds. The first were discovered in the 1930s. They become superconductors at higher temperatures than Type I superconductors, and they change into the superconducting state more gradually as their temperature falls. These are known as hard superconductors and include ceramic materials.

Ceramics are normally insulators—they do not allow an electrical current to flow through them. Most scientists had therefore ignored them as potential superconductors. In 1986, however, scientists found a ceramic compound that became a superconductor at 30K (–405°F or –243°C), which was the highest temperature by far for any superconductor at that time. This began a hunt that led to higher temperature superconductors.

Surprisingly, materials such as copper and gold, which are good conductors of electricity at room temperature, are not superconducting elements. They conduct electricity well at room temperature because they have free electrons that can move easily from atom to atom. This is not enough to make them good superconductors. Their atoms are packed so tightly together that they are unable to vibrate in the way that enables electrons to pair up and move through them without any resistance.

Supercold computers

A computer stores information in its memory by preserving thousands of on/off electrical signals. Many computer memories can work only if they are kept plugged into an electricity supply. A superconducting ring will carry a current even when there is no external power. A cryotron computer memory contains supercold rings that

carry the current to be remembered. The current flows through the device until another current is applied to clear the memory.

Superconductors can also be used to make superfast switches for computers by making use of a phenomenon called the Josephson effect, named for British scientist Brian Josephson (1940–). When two superconductors are separated by a narrow insulating gap, an electrical current flows between them across the gap. If a magnetic field is applied, the superconductivity is destroyed and the current switches off. A computer memory that uses the Josephson effect is called a Josephson memory. Josephson memories are very fast, but they are expensive because of the low temperatures needed to operate them.

See also: COMPUTER • CRYOGENICS • ELECTROMAGNETISM • LINEAR ELECTRIC MOTOR • MAGNETISM • PARTICLE ACCELERATOR • RESISTANCE • TRANSFORMER

Supersonic flight

Supersonic means faster than sound. Before the days of the jet, an airliner flight between New York and London, England, took some 13 hours. The British-French Concorde could cross the Atlantic Ocean in under three hours. For much of the flight, it cruised at more than twice the speed of sound.

The search for speed is common to all forms of transportation. Since the very beginning of powered flight in the early twentieth century, the speed of aircraft has been increased by more than one hundred times. High-speed airplanes have made the world a smaller place.

The struggle to fly ever faster and conquer the technical problems of high-speed flight gave rise to the popular notion of a sound barrier. There is in fact no such thing—it is only a side effect of supersonic flight. If a stone is dropped into water, the ripples spread out in waves. Sound works in much the same way—it is a wave disturbance in the atmosphere. The speed at which a sound wave travels depends on the temperature of the air. In a moderate climate that has an average temperature of 59°F (15°C), sound waves have a sea-level speed of 760 miles (1,225 kilometers) per hour. This speed is known to pilots as Mach 1. The unit is named after Austrian scientist Ernst Mach (1838–1916).

Supersonic, transonic, and subsonic

Mach 1 is not the same speed everywhere in the atmosphere. The speed of sound falls in colder air. Up to a ceiling of about 60,000 feet (18,000 meters), the temperature drops (to 32°F/0°C) as the altitude (height) increases and sound waves travel slower. At an altitude of 40,000 feet (12,200 meters), the speed

▶ *Models of aircraft, as well as wings for supersonic aircraft, are accurately made and tested in wind tunnels. In this free-flight training tunnel, the model is held still and air is blown past it.*

of sound is about 660 miles (1,050 kilometers) per hour. So, an airplane traveling at 1,320 miles (2,124 kilometers) per hour at this altitude is said to have a speed of Mach 2. The same aircraft flying at this speed just above the ground would have a speed of only about Mach 1.7 because sound travels faster in the warmer air near the ground.

Flight up to a speed of Mach 1 is referred to as subsonic. Flight above Mach 1 is called supersonic. Borderline speeds around Mach 1 are known as transonic. For example, some airplanes can reach Mach 1 only when they go into a dive, helped by the downward force of gravity. Speeds of Mach 5 and more are referred to as hypersonic. Large airliners like the Boeing 747 Jumbo Jet fly at high subsonic speeds in the region of Mach 0.85.

▼ *Concorde's takeoff speed was about 235 miles (375 kilometers) per hour—70 miles (110 kilometers) per hour faster than a large subsonic jet airliner. Concorde's swept-back wings were designed specifically for supersonic flight and were less efficient at takeoff speeds.*

Shock waves

When an airplane travels at low speeds, it meets very little resistance as it passes through the air. A pressure wave moving forward at the speed of sound pushes air molecules out of the way. As the speed of the airplane increases, this effect diminishes. If the airplane is traveling at Mach 1, the airplane compresses the air on contact, and a high-pressure shock wave is formed, similar to the bow wave of a ship.

The shock wave spreads out from the plane in the shape of a cone, called a Mach cone, with its point at the plane's nose. If the shock wave reaches the ground, it produces the startling sound of a loud bang, called a sonic boom.

The resistance of the air to the plane's movement increases very rapidly above Mach 1. If the plane is to travel any faster, it needs a great deal more power to overcome this drag (resistance). Shock waves also interfere with the airflow behind the plane, making it much harder to control. As a plane flies through the air, friction from air molecules heats it

◀ **NASA's experimental X-43 is a prototype for a future aircraft capable of flying at speeds up to Mach 10.**

up. This is not a problem for subsonic aircraft because the air it flies through is so cold that it counteracts the frictional heating. Supersonic planes, however, fly so fast that this heating effect can become a problem. Most planes are constructed from an aluminum alloy. This material can be used only up to speeds of about Mach 2.5 because of frictional heating. Planes designed to fly faster than this must be made of different metals, such as titanium and nickel-based alloys, that can withstand higher temperatures.

When metal is heated, it expands. The supersonic airliner Concorde grew several inches longer during a flight. Concorde's needle nose was heated more than any other part of the aircraft. Friction with the air heated it to 345°F (175°C) above the surrounding air temperature of –65°F (–55°C). As the aircraft slowed down before landing, it cooled again and shrank back to its normal length.

Supersonic wings

Wings that work very well at supersonic speeds are less efficient at low speeds, creating much drag and little lift. Designers have come up with a number of answers, such as the gracefully curving delta wing of Concorde, and the variable geometry of some fighter planes that can change the shape of their wings in flight.

Landing speeds are higher for supersonic airplanes, so longer runways must be built on airfields where they are in use.

Record breakers

The first airplane to fly supersonically was the American Bell X-1 on October 14, 1947. The first plane able to fly supersonically in level flight was the F-100 Super Sabre fighter. It set a world air speed record of 754 miles (1,215 kilometers) per hour on October 29, 1953.

The world air speed record of 2,193 miles (3,529 kilometers) per hour is held by the American Lockheed SR-71 Blackbird. Russia's MiG-25 Foxbat fighter aircraft has been tracked by radar at more than Mach 3. The fixed-wing rocket-powered X-15 U.S. research airplane flew at 4,520 miles (7,274 kilometers) per hour, equivalent to Mach 6.72, on October 3, 1967. In comparison, the rocket-powered space shuttle orbiter reenters Earth's atmosphere on its return from space at Mach 25.

There are plans to build aircraft capable of Mach 10. They will have to be built from new materials and powered by new types of engines to operate safely and reliably at such high speeds.

See also: AERODYNAMICS • AIRPLANE • SOUND

Surface tension

If a person pours a small amount of water onto a flat plate, he or she will see that it seems to curl up into a tiny ball. This happens because the outer part—the surface—of any liquid is somewhat elastic. Scientists call this effect surface tension.

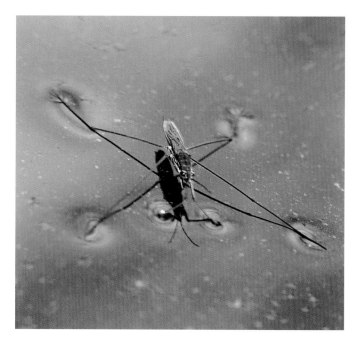

▲ *Water striders use surface tension to walk on water.*

Inside a liquid there are billions of molecules. Each molecule is attracted to all the other molecules in the liquid, and they all exert a force on each other. These forces keep the molecules of the liquid together. But this does not happen to molecules at the surface of the liquid. There are no liquid molecules above them, only at the side and below. The forces of attraction pull the top layer of molecules down toward the center of the liquid. The molecules in the top layer of the liquid are also attracted to the molecules of air or vapor above them. However, this force of attraction is just too weak to overcome the pull from the molecules within the liquid.

The force that the inside of the liquid exerts on the surface is called surface tension. It makes a kind of elastic skin on the surface of the liquid. The surface tension pulls a drop of the liquid into the shape with the smallest possible surface area, which is a sphere. Due to gravity, however, drops of liquid sitting on a surface do not form perfect spheres but are flattened slightly.

Measuring surface tension

The force of surface tension is usually measured in newtons per meter. For water, the force is about 0.07 newtons per meter. This is a very small force, but it is still enough to float a steel needle placed carefully on the water. It is also enough to support the weight of small insects, such as water striders, that rest and move on the surface of ponds. The surface tension of all liquids decreases as the temperature of the liquid increases. This is mainly because the density of vapor above a liquid increases as the liquid gets hotter and the vapor molecules have a stronger attraction for the surface molecules in the liquid. The surface tension decreases until a critical point is reached, when it drops to zero. Then the boundary between the liquid and vapor disappears.

Washing

Surface tension is also lowered when a detergent is added to water. A small amount of detergent added to the water will reduce its surface tension to the point where even a needle or a tiny insect would slip through the surface. Since the surface tension is lower, a thin film of the liquid is not as likely to become broken up by forces on the surface. Water containing detergent can therefore form large stable bubbles.

Surface tension stops water from getting to dirt on the skin and clothes. When detergent or soap is added to the water, the lowered surface tension means that the soap can surround the particles of dirt, and they can be washed away.

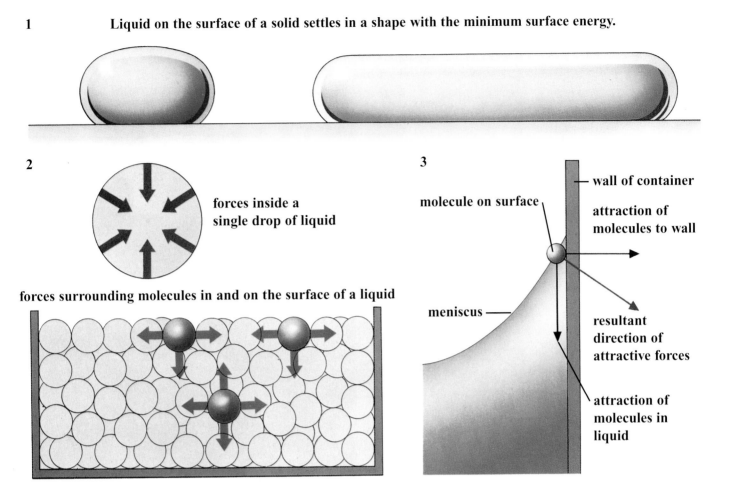

1   Liquid on the surface of a solid settles in a shape with the minimum surface energy.

2   forces inside a
single drop of liquid

forces surrounding molecules in and on the surface of a liquid

3   wall of container

molecule on surface

attraction of molecules to wall

meniscus

resultant direction of attractive forces

attraction of molecules in liquid

▲ *Surface tension makes a drop of liquid form a shape with the smallest possible surface area—a sphere. Where the effects of gravity are greater than the surface tension effects, the drop is flattened (1). The forces inside a single drop of liquid act inward from the surface. Forces are also exerted on molecules in the liquid and on its surface (2). The attraction between the wall of a container and a liquid makes the liquid curve up the side of the container (3).*

Some cleaning products, such as shampoos, detergents, windshield cleaners, washing powders, and toothpaste, contain powerful cleaners called wetting agents. These break down the surface tension of the water and allow the cleaner to get through all kinds of dirt.

Capillary action

When a liquid comes into contact with a solid, the molecules of the liquid are attracted to the molecules of the solid. This force of attraction may be greater than the force of attraction between the molecules of the liquid. This attraction is called adhesion, and it causes the surface of water to turn up where it contacts a solid such as glass. The curved surface of the water is called a meniscus.

When one end of a narrow glass tube, called a capillary tube, is dipped in water, the water rises up inside the tube. This effect is called capillary action. Surface tension tries to pull the tube downward. There is an equal upward force between the glass and the water, which pulls the water up inside the tube. The water continues rising until the surface tension forces pulling it upward are balanced by the weight of the water inside the tube. Capillary action plays an important part in raising water up the trunks of trees.

See also: ATOM AND MOLECULE • FORCES • GRAVITY • LIQUID • OSMOSIS • SOAP AND DETERGENT

Surgery

Surgery is the part of medicine that treats disease or injury by opening up the body. Diseased areas are cut out or repairs are made, and the opening is closed up. Highly trained doctors called surgeons perform the operations, which usually take place in a specially prepared room in a hospital.

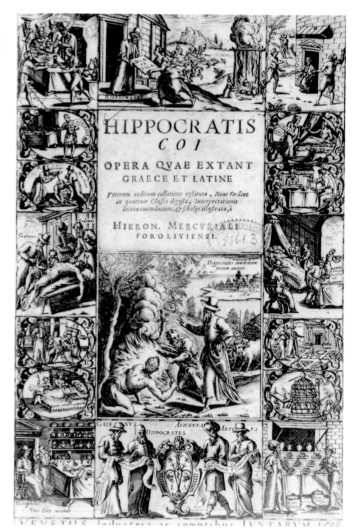

▲ *This 1588 engraving is for the title page of a book on the work of Greek scholar Hippocrates, the founding father of medicine. It shows the roles of a physician, from advice on diet and the prescription of medicines to surgery and the use of herbs in medicine.*

When a person is ill, sometimes the only way to cure the disease is by an operation. Today, people expect operations to be carried out safely and painlessly, but this was not always the case.

Until about one hundred years ago, an operation was performed with no anesthetic (a painkilling drug or gas) and with little regard for the risk of infection. Patients unlucky enough to need operations had to be held down on the operating table, and the only painkiller available was alcohol.

The surgeons had to work as quickly as possible to complete the operation. Not only were patients in pain, but many of them died from shock because they lost so much blood. If they managed to survive the operation, they often died later from infection.

Doctors now understand far more about how the body works and what causes infection. The two techniques that have completely changed surgery and have made it much safer are the use of anesthetics and the development of aseptic (germ-free) ways of operating. Surgery is now a standard part of medicine across the world.

Anesthetics

An anesthetic is a drug or gas that dulls pain. Surgery can be performed under local, regional, or general anesthetic. Local anesthetics are used to anesthetize small parts of the body. Most people have probably had a local anesthetic before a dentist filled a cavity in a tooth. The local anesthetic is usually given by injection directly into the area of surgery. It works almost immediately and prevents any feeling of pain in that area. The effects of a local anesthetic wear off in a few hours.

Regional anesthetics numb or deaden an entire region of the body by injecting an anesthetic in one of several ways, depending on the type of surgery being performed. These methods include injecting close to a large nerve, injecting directly into the area of the operation, and injecting into the spine in a procedure called spinal anesthesia.

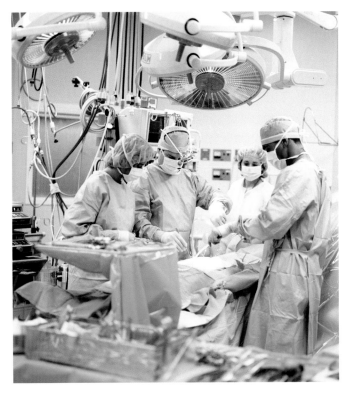

▶ *Surgeons in a modern operating room are clothed in sterile gowns and surrounded by filtered, sterile air.*

A patient is given a general anesthetic either by injection or by inhaling (breathing in) anesthetic gases. Apart from being unable to feel pain, the patient falls quickly into a very deep sleep and cannot move. Patients are completely unaware of the surgery, and on gradually waking from the anesthetic, they often do not realize that the operation has been performed.

Using anesthetics to eliminate pain, as well as tools to prevent blood loss, means that surgeons do not have to hurry or rush through an operation. They can take whatever time is needed.

Cleaner operations

French chemist Louis Pasteur (1822–1895) discovered that certain types of bacteria could transmit disease. Working on these ideas, English surgeon Joseph Lister (1827–1912) developed the use of antiseptics in surgery. Earlier, operations were carried out in a large room with an audience. The term *operating theater* came from this practice—people watched the operations as if they were at a play in the theater. The surgeon would take off his coat and put on a robe. He did not wear rubber gloves and did not sterilize his instruments. Naturally, all surgical wounds became infected afterward.

Lister found that spraying an antiseptic called carbolic acid on and around the wound during the operation reduced the chance of an infection developing later. This discovery led to the modern methods of aseptic surgery. Antiseptic surgery killed the bacteria around the wound. Aseptic surgery keeps bacteria from getting to the wound in the first place. In aseptic surgery, all the instruments used are sterilized, the surgeon wears a sterilized gown and gloves, and the parts of the patient not involved in the operation are covered with sterile drapes. The open wound has little chance of coming into contact with bacteria.

Operations such as those to repair hernias (stitching loose muscles into place) have little chance of infection. Operations such as removing an appendix still carry a risk of infection from the bacteria within a patient. With modern drugs, even this infection rate has been reduced dramatically.

The operating room

Hospital operating rooms must always be kept completely aseptic. A transfer area from the general wards helps to prevent bacteria from entering the operating room.

All operations require pure air to eliminate the chance that an infection might be carried in with the patient. Modern surgery rooms have filters to clean the air entering and exiting the operating area. More advanced systems enclose the surgical team and patient in a column of clean, filtered air.

During surgery, the patient lies on an operating table. Initially, these tables were wooden but have since evolved to sophisticated pieces of machinery that can be adjusted electronically to suit the patient and the operation being performed.

Surgical instruments

Many instruments now in use were developed more than one hundred years ago. Although there have been modifications and new developments, the basic types of instruments have stayed the same. The surgeon uses a variety of scissors and scalpels. A scalpel is a specially shaped cutting tool with a stainless steel blade clipped on to a solid metal handle. The blade can be changed to suit the type of incision (cut) the surgeon has to make.

Hemostats are instruments used to stop the blood supply to an artery or vein before it is cut. The vessel is clipped in two places and can then be cut between the clips without any great loss of blood. Forceps resemble scissors with "jaws" on the end and are used for grasping or holding firmly.

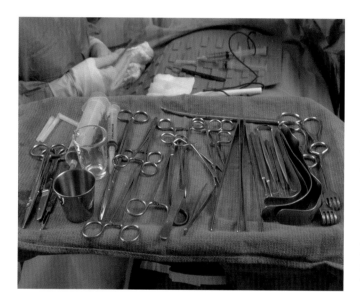

Surgeons also use tools called retractors to hold an incision open during an operation. They may be held by an assistant or fixed in place. Countless other instruments are used for various specialized operations. It is now common for operating rooms to have previously prepared packs of sterilized instruments ready for a particular operation.

Stitches

There are several different types of stitches that a surgeon can use to sew up a wound. They can be divided into two basic types—those that dissolve naturally in the body tissue after several days and those that have to be removed some time after the operation. Sometimes the surgeon will close up a wound using clips. These look something like large staples and must be removed by a doctor or nurse when the wound starts to heal.

A surgeon's role

A doctor who performs operations is called a surgeon. Today, surgeons are qualified doctors who have gone on to more specialized training. Years ago, this was not the case. At one time, barbers performed surgery. The barber pole, with its red and white stripes, is supposed to be a symbol of a bandage and blood.

▲ *The instruments necessary for each operation are laid out ready for use. After each operation, they are taken away and sterilized at a high temperature to kill disease-causing bacteria and viruses.*

▶ *Keyhole surgery involves carrying out operations by inserting instruments through small incisions in the skin. Avoiding the use of large incisions reduces the risk of infection and speeds the patient's recovery.*

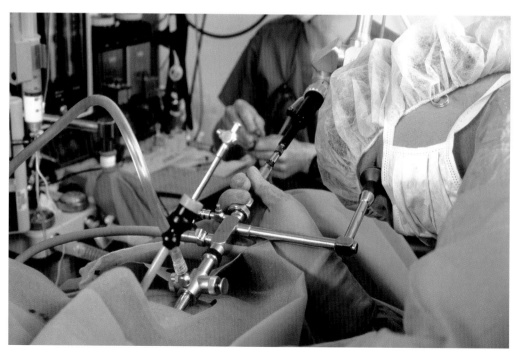

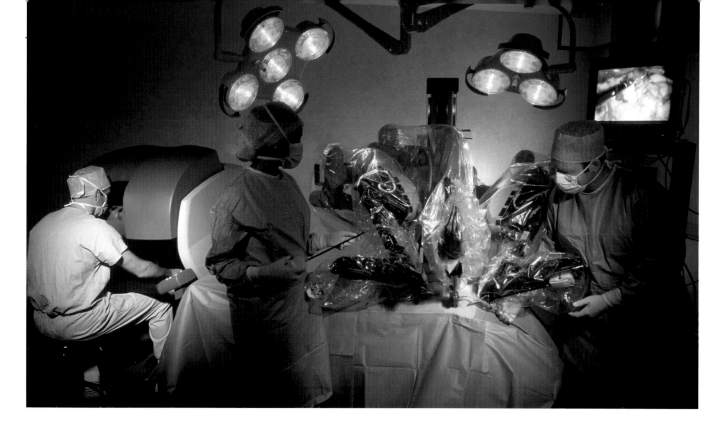

After receiving a degree from medical school, the would-be surgeon must study and train for up to five years, and sometimes longer. During that time, the doctor learns the techniques of surgery and identifies a particular field of surgery in which he or she would like to specialize. This is done by observing, by assisting at operations, and by performing surgery under the supervision of an experienced surgeon. The doctor must then pass an examination to be certified as a practicing surgeon.

A patient is referred to a surgeon when a doctor thinks that the person's condition might need treatment by surgery. During the initial examination, the surgeon performs a thorough medical checkup to ensure that surgery is indeed necessary. He or she then plans the type of operation that will best cure the condition. After the operation, the surgeon

DID YOU KNOW?

Lasers (devices producing concentrated beams of light) are increasingly used in surgery as scalpels and to seal cut blood vessels. They are also used to remove various skin blemishes and to help correct some defects of vision.

▲ *Medical robots help surgeons in the operating theater. Unlike a human surgeon, a robot can have several hands, which are manipulated by human surgeons using computerized controls.*

monitors the patient to ensure that there are no complications and that the person will have a normal recovery.

Scanners

In recent years, many instruments and surgical techniques have been developed to help surgeons prepare and carry out operations. Developed at the beginning of the twentieth century, X-ray imaging revolutionized surgery, enabling surgeons to look inside a patient's body before surgery. X-rays are still used extensively. During operations, they are sometimes used to check on the position of an instrument within the body.

Scanners developed since the 1970s provide even more detailed images of the body's interior and help surgeons plan complex surgery before opening up the patient.

Reducing bleeding

Cutting a patient's body inevitably causes bleeding, and surgeons strive to keep this to a minimum. Apart from the danger to the patient of losing blood, the surgeon must have a clear view of the operation site, which can be obscured by blood leaking from vessels.

Incisions are kept as small as possible, and leaking blood vessels are cauterized (sealed by heat). A branch of surgery called keyhole surgery avoids large incisions altogether. Instruments as thin as a pencil are passed through small holes in the skin. A probe shows the surgeon the view inside the body on a screen. Other structures can be viewed and operated on using an endoscope—a flexible glass-fiber tube that transmits light and is fitted with a camera and tiny cutting tools. An endoscope is passed along a tube such as the windpipe or esophagus, and no incision is made.

Microsurgery

Some structures in the body are so small that a microscope is necessary to see them in sufficient detail to operate on them. The bones of the inner and middle ear and the smallest nerves and blood vessels are examples. Microsurgery is a modern branch of surgery that deals with the repair of these tiny structures.

> **DID YOU KNOW?**
>
> Techniques for transplanting the human heart were developed in the United States in the late 1950s, but the first successful heart transplant was not performed until 1967 by South African surgeon Christiaan Barnard (1922–2001).

Transplant surgery

It is now possible to replace diseased or damaged parts of the human body, either with healthy parts removed from other people or with artificial parts made from plastics and metal. The body treats transplanted parts as foreign invaders, just like germs, and rejects them. The greatest challenge with transplant surgery is preventing the body from rejecting its new parts.

When a diseased organ is to be replaced with a healthy living organ, as little time as possible—a few hours at most—must pass between removing the organ from the donor (the living or dead person from whom the organ is taken) and putting it into the recipient's body.

◀ *Surgeons spend long hours watching and assisting more experienced surgeons. They can also watch operations that are relayed by video from almost anywhere in the world by telephone or the Internet, or that have been recorded for repeated viewing.*

▶ *A person with a diseased kidney is having her blood purified by a dialysis machine. As soon as a suitable donor is found, a surgeon will remove the patient's diseased kidney and replace it with a healthy one. Transplant surgery can transform a patient's life. Patients who previously had to be connected to a dialysis machine for hours at a time to purify their blood, or who could not walk more than a few steps due to heart disease, are able to live nearly normal lives after organ transplants.*

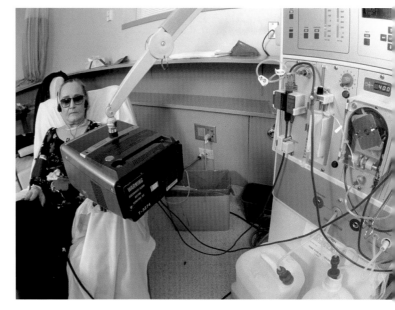

When a healthy organ replaces a diseased organ, the body of the recipient (the person receiving the new organ) must be made unable to reject it. This is done by matching the donor organ with the recipient closely at the cellular level and by using anti-rejection drugs called immunosuppressants.

However, immunosuppressive drugs reduce the rejection of all foreign material—including disease-causing bacteria and viruses. Thus, the person loses much of the ability to fight infection.

The long road to success

The first successful transplant surgery was that of a kidney from a young man to his twin brother, which took place in Boston in 1954. Since the two men were twins, there was no problem of rejection. A kidney from a twin or closely matched family member is the ideal transplant, but the use of a kidney from an unrelated person has become widespread, thanks to immunosuppressive drugs.

The first single human lung transplant was performed by Dr. James D. Hardy of the University of Mississippi in 1963, but the patient died within days. Most surgeons now transplant the heart and lungs combined. The liver and the pancreas have also been transplanted. Once-incurable diseases of the blood and some types of immune deficiency can be treated with bone marrow transplants.

Strides have been made in the field of orthopedic surgery as well; in 1987 a knee taken from a man killed in an accident was successfully transplanted into the leg of a woman at the Hospital of the University of Pennsylvania. Surgeons also routinely replace diseased hip and knee joints with new joints made from plastic and metal.

Robotic surgery

Robotic surgery is becoming increasingly common in the operating theater. Robots are used for some operations because they can hold instruments more steadily and move them more precisely than a human surgeon. A system called Robodoc was first tried in 1992 in an operation to replace an artificial hip and has since been used in thousands of hip-replacement operations. Robodoc drills the holes that receive the new hip more accurately than a human surgeon.

A robotic system called da Vinci is used in a wide variety of surgical procedures. The surgeon operates hand controllers at a console in the operating theater. The controllers then move the instruments that actually carry out the operation. About one hundred da Vinci robots are in use throughout the United States, Europe, and Asia. The surgeon and the robot are normally separated by just a few feet, but they could be much farther apart—perhaps not even in the same country. In 2001, surgeons used a robot to remove a patient's gallbladder—the surgeons were in New York and the robot and patient were in Strasbourg, France.

See also: ANESTHETIC • ANTIBIOTIC • BACTERIA • LASER • MEDICAL IMAGING • MEDICAL TECHNOLOGY

Surveying

Land surveying is the measuring of distances and angles on Earth's surface to make maps. In developed countries, surveyors work to keep existing maps up to date. In developing countries, there are still large areas that have never been mapped in detail.

There are two main types of surveying. Geodetic surveying takes into account that Earth's surface is curved. Geodetic surveys are used for large areas, such as islands and countries. For small areas, surveyors can assume that they are measuring a flat surface. This type of surveying is called plane surveying.

The first stage in any survey is to measure as accurately as possible the distances and angles between a series of points. These are called the primary control points, and other points are measured in relation to them. The primary control points are arranged in a series of triangles, and surveying methods are based on simple geometry.

For example, if the lengths of the three sides of a triangle are known, the angles in that triangle can be calculated. So to survey an oblong field with straight sides, one needs only to measure the lengths of the four sides and one diagonal (the line joining two opposite corners). The diagonal divides the field into two triangles. This method of surveying, which does not require any measurement of angles, is called trilateration.

Triangulation

Another method does involve the measurement of angles. When the length of one side of a triangle and all three angles are known, the lengths of the other two sides can be calculated. This method is called triangulation. In the past, all large-scale surveys were based on the triangulation method, and it remains the chief surveying method today.

▲ *This sixteenth-century illustration shows the lines of sight of engineers using surveying instruments of the time. In Europe, surveying made great leaps forward during the Renaissance.*

Measurement of a base line is the first stage in triangulation. This base line forms the basis of the survey, and so it must be measured as accurately as possible. This was traditionally done by means of metal measuring tapes. The best tapes are made of invar (an alloy of nickel and steel), which does not expand and contract with changing temperature as much as other metals. Base lines are often several miles long, and measurements with invar tapes are slow. Corrections must be made not only for temperature, but also for the slope of the land. These corrections are necessary because maps must accurately show the horizontal distances between points, not the longer lengths that would be found by measuring up and down slopes.

The ends of the base line are usually marked by concrete pillars sunk into the ground, as are the other primary control points. When the base line has been measured, distances to a third point can be found simply by measuring the angles between the two points at the end of the base line and the third point. Angular measurements are then used to measure the positions of all the other control points in the network. Sometimes an extra base line is measured in a distant part of the network to check the accuracy of the survey.

The chief instrument used in triangulation is the theodolite. This instrument has a spirit level that enables it to be set up horizontally on a tripod. It has a telescope that turns both horizontally and vertically. Inside the instrument are fine divisions that enable surveyors to measure horizontal and vertical angles. Most theodolites measure angles to within about one second of arc, or $\frac{1}{3,600}$th of a degree (there are 60 seconds in one minute and 60 minutes in one degree).

DID YOU KNOW?

Surveying probably began in ancient Egypt about five thousand years ago. The Great Pyramid of Khufu at Giza shows evidence of advanced surveying expertise. Built in about 2700 BCE, the massive stone structure, originally standing 471 feet (143 meters) high and weighing 5¾ million tons (5.2 million tonnes), has an almost perfectly square base with sides aligned north-south and east-west.

Until recently, trilateration was far too slow for use in large-scale surveys. After World War II (1939–1945), several instruments were invented that measure the time taken for electromagnetic radiation to travel between two points. Geodimeters, which send out beams of light, are used for distances up to 15 miles (24 kilometers). Tellurometers, which measure the time taken for a radar signal to echo back from a target, are used for distances up to 40 miles (64 kilometers).

◄ *One of the most useful surveying tools is the spirit level. When a bubble sits precisely in the middle of a sealed, fluid-filled tube or dish, the instrument is level.*

▲ *Satellite positioning, laser range finders, and aerial photography are used to measure the height of mountains, such as the Matterhorn in Switzerland, which at 14,690 feet (4,478 meters) is one of Europe's highest peaks.*

Measuring heights

If a surveyor knows the distance between two points and the vertical angle between them, he or she can figure out the difference in height between the two points. Hence, theodolites can be used to measure heights. However, such measurements are not accurate enough to fix the heights of control points. For this purpose, a telescopic instrument called a transit is used. When the telescope is exactly horizontal, the surveyor reads the measurement on a staff, graduated in feet and inches, which is placed on a second point. The difference between the height of the telescope and the reading on the staff is the height difference between the two points, which is easy to measure.

▲ *A surveyor uses a theodolite at a construction site to map the land. The theodolite is clamped onto a tripod and leveled with leveling screws. The instrument is rotated horizontally, and the telescope is pointed at survey stations. The horizontal and vertical angles are then read through the scale-reading eyepiece.*

Electronic distance measurers (EDMs), or laser range finders, have become standard tools in modern surveying on construction sites, largely replacing tape measures. A laser beam is sent out from a laser fixed to the theodolite to a prism reflector held some distance away. The system then automatically calculates the precise distance between the theodolite and the reflector by measuring the time taken for the laser to transmit a signal to the reflector and return.

Filling in the details

When the network of points has been accurately measured, the latitudes and longitudes of the points are fixed. Traditionally, this was done by making observations of stars. Now, locations are accurately determined by means of satellite positioning. Then the surveyors begin the task of filling in the details between the control points. They start this by fixing secondary points. From these points, surveyors may measure a series of distances and angles along a zigzag line. This process is called traversing. As they proceed, they also measure all the details of the land, such as the positions of fields, houses, and roads, together with the heights of the various points. This information is recorded and later plotted onto a map.

Another method of location is plane table surveying, which involves mounting a drawing board on a tripod and then plotting the details of the land around fixed points.

Tachymetry involves the use of a theodolite with two short horizontal marks above and below the central horizontal line. These extra lines are placed so that when a measuring staff is sighted, the difference between the upper and lower readings on the staff represents a fraction (usually one hundredth) of the distance to the staff. If the readings are 6 feet and 4 feet (1.8 and 1.2 meters), for example, the difference between the viewer and the staff is about 200 feet (63 meters).

In large-scale mapping, these methods have been replaced to a great extent by mapping from photographs taken from airplanes and satellites.

These photographs are taken in long strips, and each photograph overlaps the next by about 60 percent. These overlapping areas can be viewed through a stereoscope so that they appear as a three-dimensional model. As a result, the photographs enable mapmakers not only to measure distances and plot land features, but also to calculate the heights of points on the land.

Modern surveying

The use of laser range finders, satellite-positioning systems, and theodolites with built-in computers has made surveying faster and more accurate than was previously possible. In the past, readings taken from a theodolite were noted by hand and then copied or rekeyed every time they were needed for calculation. Now the readings can be entered into a dedicated surveying system, and every time they are needed, the readings can be transferred digitally, thus removing the opportunity for introduction of errors in calculations.

Data can be transferred over long distances accurately and quickly by means of the Internet. On construction sites, survey data can even be used to control the movements of earthmoving machines that level the ground before construction begins, ensuring a perfectly level site.

The use of common standards throughout the surveying, engineering, architectural, and construction industries means that they can share and transfer data easily. Survey and building data can now be combined with satellite or aerial photography to produce highly detailed, three-dimensional, digital models of construction sites and larger areas.

◀ *An aerial photograph of New York City shows Manhattan in the center. Aerial photography revolutionized mapping. Photographic images of complex sites such as towns can replace the laborious process of surveying on the ground between and around all the obstacles such as buildings.*

See *also:* BUILDING TECHNIQUES • MAPMAKING • MATHEMATICS • RADAR

Suspension

In the days of the horse and cart, travel was very uncomfortable, not only because of bumpy roads. Axles (the rods connecting pairs of wheels) were fixed rigidly to the frame of the carriage. Modern systems of springs and shock absorbers—collectively called suspension—makes an automobile ride much smoother.

The first automobiles followed the same designs that had been used for carriages. They had narrow tires and simple leaf springs—strips of springy steel bracketed together. Modern cars have complex suspension systems that cushion the passengers from shock and also ensure that the wheels stay in contact with the road. Safe acceleration, braking, and cornering depend on the car's suspension system.

Tires

Pneumatic (air-filled) tires may be said to be part of the suspension system in that they protect the car and passengers against bumps and jolts. A tire is itself a form of spring. The first pneumatic tire was patented in Scotland as early as 1845, but the first real development came with the work of Scottish inventor John Boyd Dunlop (1840–1921). He designed a tire for his son's tricycle that absorbed some of the shock from the road. Dunlop realized that a pneumatic tire made the ride more comfortable and the vehicle easier to move along.

Springs and shock absorbers

Tires alone cannot provide enough cushioning. It is necessary to have springs between the wheels and the body of the car. One type is the leaf spring. It

▶ *A car's suspension system lets the wheels move up and down to stay in contact with rough ground, while the car's body travels along more smoothly.*

provides cushioning and also serves to locate the axle to secure it in a position that allows only up-and-down motion. Another common type of spring is the coil spring—a steel spiral. If a spring is to act smoothly, it needs some kind of damper or shock absorber. Without this, a jolt might start the spring bouncing like a trampoline. As well as being uncomfortable, this could be dangerous because it might make the wheels leave the road.

Shock absorbers usually work by hydraulics, using the action of a liquid. Inside a sealed cylinder there is a sliding piston. One end is attached to the chassis and the other to the axle. The cylinder is filled with oil. Holes in the piston allow the oil to seep through as it moves, and this effectively cushions any shocks. Some designs use a gas rather than a liquid. In this case, the shock absorber can act as a spring as well.

Air and other gases can provide a cushioned bed for the chassis. Air springs are like balloons. They make very good springs but cannot secure the axle in position. Air springs come in two basic types—high pressure and low pressure. A low-pressure system will operate at around 70 pounds per square

INDEPENDENT COIL SPRING SUSPENSION

car body

coil spring and damper unit

swing axle

▲ *The swing axle of this vehicle has its own coil-spring suspension.*

HYDRAULIC SHOCK ABSORBER

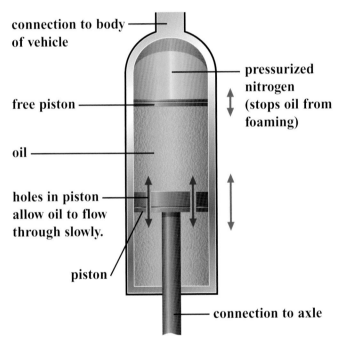

connection to body of vehicle

free piston

oil

holes in piston allow oil to flow through slowly.

piston

pressurized nitrogen (stops oil from foaming)

connection to axle

▲ *A hydraulic shock absorber consists of a piston inside a sealed cylinder. The piston is connected to the axle, and the cylinder is connected to the vehicle's body. The cylinder is full of oil, and the piston has holes in it. When the axle moves up or down, the piston moves through the oil and absorbs some of the axle's movement energy.*

inch (4.9 kilograms per square centimeter); a high-pressure system can handle up to ten times as much load. One system of this kind takes the form of a metal sphere that is divided by a flexible partition—a diaphragm. On one side of the diaphragm is oil, and on the other side is gas. A

TORSION-BAR SPRING

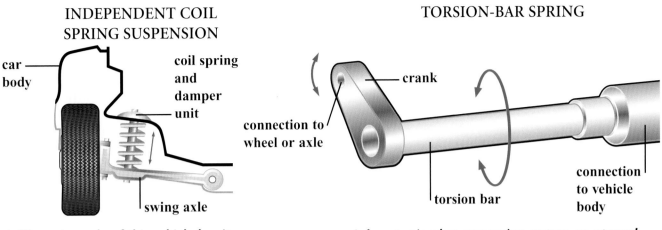

crank

connection to wheel or axle

torsion bar

connection to vehicle body

▲ *In a torsion bar suspension system, an upward movement of the wheel makes the torsion bar twist. The bar tries to resist the twisting motion, making it behave like a spring.*

piston linked to the wheel acts on the oil, which compresses the gas and provides the spring action. A similar system makes use of a different fluid—a mixture of water and antifreeze. Its hydraulic system follows a different design; it is cheaper but not self-leveling.

Axles

The design of an axle is crucial to the safety of the vehicle and to its road handling. The traditional solid beam axle is still in common use, both in the front (common on trucks) and at the rear. Methods of location other than leaf springs include trailing arms, Panhard rods, and Watts linkage.

The solid beam axle is good in that it keeps the wheels rigidly upright and corners well. Its disadvantage is that it is heavy and that a jolt to one wheel will affect the other. Other designs allow independent suspension. The swing axle, used for years on the Volkswagen "Beetle," is a beam axle divided in half. The twin wishbone is a common method of independent suspension. It has a compact design allowing excellent steering and a tight turning radius. Other systems include the MacPherson strut, which uses the damper-coil unit for securing, the semitrailing arm, and the De Dion System.

See also: AUTOMOBILE • BEARING • BRAKE SYSTEM • HYDRAULICS • SPRING

Switch

A switch is a device that allows people to control electricity. Switches start or stop the current from flowing in an electric circuit. In the home, school, and office they are used to turn on or off electric lights, heaters, vacuum cleaners, radios, televisions, computers, and many other electrical items.

Switches come in all shapes and sizes, but most consist of two metal contacts that come together for the "on" position and are pulled apart for the "off" position.

Safety in switches

Switches are designed to stand up to more current than should normally flow through them. For example, if there is a short circuit, a switch normally carrying a small amount of current may have to carry a very heavy load, if only for a few thousandths of a second. If the switch fails, a serious accident could happen.

The domestic electricity supply is 120 volts. This voltage could give anyone a bad shock, so switches must be well insulated—a current must not flow through the parts that can be touched. Some switches are worked by a pull cord, which is safer because the switch can be operated without having to touch it.

Types of switch

The type of contact used in a switch depends on where the switch will be used. The knife blade contact is used in switches where the starting current of the device is not high compared to its working current. The moving contact is the knife blade and is usually made of copper.

A butt contact is used in a switch where the starting current is high compared to the working current, such as in electric motors. Some switches

work automatically and are controlled by heat or light. Time switches are controlled by clocks. They can be made to turn on and off at preset times. A thermostat in an oven, an engine cooling system, or a central heating system is a switch that goes on and off depending on the temperature.

Thyristor

A thyristor is a device that will let electricity flow in one direction but not in the opposite direction. To let any electricity flow through a thyristor, it must be switched on with a second small voltage. Thyristors are used as switches, the small voltage being used to switch on a much larger voltage.

A thyristor is a type of diode or silicon-controlled rectifier (SCR); it converts alternating current (AC) to direct current (DC). It is made from a four-layer

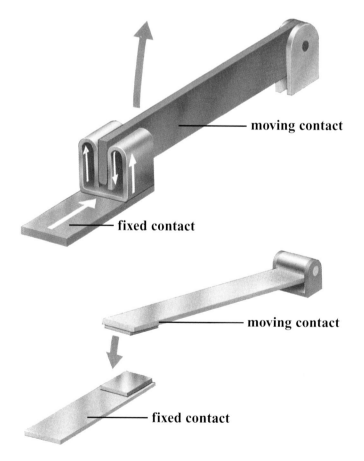

moving contact

fixed contact

moving contact

fixed contact

▲ *These illustrations show a knife blade contact set (top) and a butt contact set (bottom).*

sandwich of semiconductor material and is based on the technology of the transistor. A thyristor has three terminals: an anode, which is connected to one of the outer layers of the sandwich; a cathode, which is connected to the other outer layer; and a gate, which is connected to one of the inner layers.

In a thyristor, electricity will not flow from the cathode to the anode and will only flow from the anode to the cathode if a small voltage is applied to the gate. Once the gate voltage has switched it on, the thyristor continues to conduct electricity in one direction until the voltage is reversed or the voltage becomes very small.

Uses of thyristors

Thyristors are switches used as controllers in many electrical circuits. The most important application of thyristors is in circuits with AC. This electricity flows first in one direction, then in the opposite direction, then in the first direction, and so on. This change in direction of flow of electricity occurs many times a second.

If a thyristor is placed in a circuit carrying AC, it will let current through only in one direction and only when it has been switched on by a small gate voltage. If the point at which the trigger voltage applied to the thyristor is varied, then the thyristor can be made to conduct electricity for a longer or shorter period. The earlier the trigger pulse, the larger will be the amount of electrical power allowed through the thyristor.

Thyristors can therefore be used not only as switches—the small trigger pulse switching on the main circuit—but also to vary the power in the main AC circuit. They are often used in televisions, light dimmers, and even in large machines such as

▲ *Computer chips contain microscopic electronic components that work as switches. Millions of them control the flow of electrical currents through computers and other digital electronic systems.*

electric locomotives. They are used as switches for large currents because they do not produce damaging arcs (sparks) in the same way as mechanical switches.

See also: BATTERY • COMPUTER • ELECTRIC CIRCUIT • ELECTRICITY • INSULATOR • MICROELECTRONICS • SEMICONDUCTOR • SOLENOID • THERMOSTAT

Tank

A tank is an armored vehicle that travels on continuous tracks and has a large gun built into it. Tanks can travel over rough, hilly, soft, or wet ground very easily and are difficult for an enemy to stop. They usually fight in large groups against other tanks.

The name "tank" was first used by the British, who introduced these vehicles during World War I (1914–1918). When the first models were secretly being built, the workers in the factories making them were told that the vehicles were special movable storage tanks for supplying water to troops in the desert.

Although very slow and clumsy by today's standards, the tanks of 1916 proved very effective against machine guns and barbed wire. (Such defenses made infantry movements difficult and costly in lives during that war.) In fact, the tanks were sometimes so effective that they outpaced their supporting infantry—which had to follow immediately behind if the breakthrough was to be successful and maintained.

At the Battle of Cambrai in France in 1917 British tanks overwhelmed the surprised Germans, rolling forward and making a huge breach in their defenses. However, the advantage of surprise was lost within days because of inadequate backup forces, and the Germans soon counterattacked, regaining much of their lost ground. Although the use of tanks at Cambrai ended in a stalemate, that early success convinced military commanders on both sides of the value of tanks. They have played an important part in wars and military confrontations ever since.

The early tanks that saw action in World War I moved no faster than a walking pace, had only small 6-pound (2.7 kilogram) guns or machine guns, and were always breaking down. After World War I, more powerful and reliable engines were built, changing slow, awkward assault vehicles into faster and more maneuverable fighting machines that were capable of speeds up to 30 miles per hour (50 kilometers per hour).

Major tank battles

It was in World War II (1939–1945) that tanks were first used on a really large scale. The Germans even developed a new style of warfare they called *Blitzkrieg* (lightning war), using tanks and airplanes to overwhelm their enemies by surprise. Poland, France, and Russia all suffered heavy losses from Blitzkrieg attacks in the early part of the war.

In 1943, however, the Germans lost a major battle to Soviet tanks at Kursk in Russia. This was the biggest tank battle ever fought up to that time. Large tank battles were also being fought in North Africa in desert conditions that required special skill. After the Allied invasion of German-occupied Europe in 1944, the use of tanks was vital in the push toward Germany and the final Allied victory.

In the latter part of the twentieth century, tanks were a deciding factor in the Middle East wars between Israel and its Arab neighbors and between

▲ *The first tanks, such as the one in this photograph, rolled on the battlefield during World War I. At first they did little more than provide cover for advancing infantry troops.*

▶ *Tanks can cross trenches up to about 9 feet (2.7 meters) wide, but temporary bridges are sometimes laid for tanks to cross wider gaps.*

coalition forces and Iraq. Modern tanks are divided into two categories. Main battle tanks, such as the German Leopard 2, British Challenger 2, and American M1 Abrams, are heavily armored tanks specially designed to fight other tanks. Armored reconnaissance vehicles, such as the British Scorpion, are smaller, lighter tanks. These are built to seek out and harass an enemy's strongpoints and to test their defenses.

In many ways, a modern tank looks like earlier ones. It still runs on continuous tracks, usually has one major weapon, and relies on metal armor for protection. However, there have been many changes and improvements over the years. Since a tank is basically a mobile gun platform, the two most important areas of change have been in maneuverability (the ability to move about) and weapons. More powerful engines have produced

tanks that can travel at speeds up to about 45 miles (70 kilometers) per hour and can turn full circle on the spot. The weaponry of a tank can vary considerably, depending on what it is required to do. Most battle tanks have a main gun with a caliber of 4 inches (120 millimeters) or more.

Design

A tank usually has a main body, called the hull, with a rotating turret mounted on top. The hull is supported on a wheeled suspension system that runs on linked tracks. Inside the hull sits the driver, together with most of the ammunition, the motor, transmission, and fuel. In the turret are the weapons, some ammunition, night fighting and communications equipment, along with the commander, the gunner, and the loader. In some tanks, such as the French Leclerc and Russian T-90 main battle tanks, a mechanized autoloader has rendered the loader unnecessary. In smaller tanks and armored reconnaissance vehicles, there may be just two crew members in the turret.

Ever since tanks were first used against other tanks, and specially designed "tank-busting" guns and missiles were developed, designers have concentrated on reducing the tank's silhouette, or,

DID YOU KNOW?

The front of the American Abrams tank is so low, in order to make the tank a smaller target, that the driver is practically lying on his back when operating the vehicle.

in other words, making a tank appear smaller to the enemy. Obviously, the smaller a tank looks, the harder it will be to hit.

As tank warfare becomes more complicated, the variety and amount of special equipment needed onboard a modern battle tank increases. Apart from the main weapons and ammunition, there is often a variety of extra machine guns, rocket, grenade, and smoke canister launchers, antinuclear or biochemical filters, and missile systems. These devices need guidance and control equipment of their own.

In addition, there may be a number of sighting systems for the main gun. Optical telescope sights were the most common way of aiming until the 1960s, but then very accurate laser range finders

▼ *A tank's turret is a hot and cramped workplace. In combat, with the hatches closed, the crew views the world outside through viewing ports and periscopes. Computer screens show position and target information.*

were developed. During World War II, tank combat would usually end once night fell because neither side could see the enemy. Postwar scientific achievements in producing infrared and other night vision systems allow modern tanks to fight at night or in dense fog or smoke.

One way to reduce the amount of space and therefore the silhouette of a tank is to remove the turret altogether. Sweden produced a turretless tank called the Stridsvagn 103. To move the gun from side to side, the whole tank must turn. A complex hydropneumatic suspension system, using a combination of air and fluid pressure, raises or lowers the hull and the gun fixed to it. The Stridsvagn has a retractable (it can be drawn in) bulldozer shovel on the front, so that it can dig itself into the ground and wait in ambush for the approaching enemy.

Tanks are not fuel-efficient vehicles, and in battle, fuel supplies are often hard to maintain. Most tanks are powered by diesel engines, but the American

▲ **Tanks played a prominent role in both Gulf wars against Iraq. The American Abrams tanks were the fastest and deadliest on the battlefield.**

M1 Abrams tank is powered by a gas turbine engine. This powerful 1,500-horsepower motor is based on jet airplane engines. It can run equally efficiently on gasoline, diesel, or jet fuels—only one of which may be available in a particular combat area.

Basic armor

Because tanks are so large and such easy targets, they need the protection of thick armor plating. But it is not only thickness that makes armor protective. For some time, antitank guns fired high-velocity (high-speed) shells to pierce tank armor. To prevent this, tank manufacturers use a special alloy called nickel-chrome steel, which does not crack easily. Also, the armor is slanted to deflect high-velocity shells that always arrive on a flat trajectory (level with the ground).

Battle experience has shown that tanks are usually hit on the front of the hull and turret. So the thickest armor and most sharply angled surfaces are at the front of the vehicle. The rest of the tank is less heavily armored, in order to save weight and improve mobility.

Although slanting steel armor is very effective against ordinary high-velocity rounds, it is vulnerable to other antitank shells. A high-explosive antitank (HEAT) shell contains a shaped charge that explodes close to the tank's armor. Hot, concentrated gases from the explosion melt a hole through the armor, and the liquid metal flies into the tank. High-explosive squash heads (HESH) are shells that explode against armor on a delayed fuse. This delay, though only very slight, sets up shock waves that shatter the armor inside, sending a deadly hail of sharp steel fragments flying around the tank's interior.

These chemical-energy warheads are best when fired at slow speed. They must be aimed high, so they curve down through the air onto the target and are not deflected by sloping surfaces.

New armor technology

Because HEAT and HESH shells are so effective against nickel-chrome steel plate, it has been necessary to develop special armor. A double thickness of armor, with an air gap between, is one answer. The advantage is that the effect of the HEAT or HESH shell can be absorbed by the outer layer, while the inner layer protects the crew in the tank. Its chief disadvantages are added weight and reduced mobility.

To use the advantages of all the different types of armor, the latest tanks are being produced with a new composite armor made from a secret combination of steel, plastic, and air gaps. The best-known is the British-made Chobham armor that is fitted to the Leopard 2 and M1 Abrams tanks. It is believed that Russia has created a similar armor.

Surprisingly, another type of armor, explosive reactive armor (ERA), is designed to explode when a shell hits it. It is made from a layer of explosive between steel plates. When a shaped-charge shell hits a tank, the armor explodes outward and stops the charge from penetrating the tank.

Armor may also offer protection against some effects of nuclear warfare. Obviously, no tank could survive a nuclear missile strike, but it is possible to survive the effects of smaller nuclear shells. Both the blast and the heat are largely deflected by the

DID YOU KNOW?

The American Abrams tank is one of the heaviest main battle tanks. It weighs 69.5 tons (63 tonnes).

armor. Most tanks are virtually sealed from the outside world once the hatches are closed. All modern battle tanks also have some sort of filtering system, to guard against the threat of radioactive fallout dust or poison gas.

Weapons

When the first tanks rolled out across no-man's-land during World War I, a machine gun or two mounted in the side were usually enough, because no similar opposition was expected. The main purpose of the tank at that time was simply to provide protection against enemy machine guns and to cut through or roll over barbed-wire defenses. The guns were useful to deal with any foot soldiers foolhardy enough to try to stop the lumbering monster. In some cases, heavier guns like 6-pounders (2.7 kilograms) were used to discourage enemy field artillery.

In time and with prolonged battle experience, it became clear that the best defense against a tank is another tank, and so the need for more powerful guns began to grow. Most modern battle tanks are built with a 4-inch (120-millimeter) main gun with much the same hitting power as a medium-sized artillery piece.

Yet in an age of missiles, tanks are still armed with guns similar to the weapons carried in World War II, mainly because of the ammunition. A missile has normally just one kind of warhead. A tank gunner has a choice of four or five different rounds to deal with each target that presents itself. These weapons may include HEAT and HESH rounds, conventional armor-piercing shells, armor-

◄ *Lightweight fighting vehicles are being built in a factory. A tank's hull is made from steel plates up to 12 inches (30 centimeters) thick.*

▲ **The American Abrams tank is one of the most advanced tanks in the world. Its laser range finder and computerized systems enable it to hit six targets within 60 seconds at a range of up to 2¹/₂ miles (4 kilometers).**

piercing discarding-sabots (APDS shells can penetrate armor several times as thick as the caliber of the gun itself), or in certain circumstances even small nuclear warheads.

Beside knocking out other tanks and armored vehicles, a battle tank needs to defend itself against smaller enemies. Infantry can be particularly dangerous, attacking from very close range with grenades and antitank rockets and missiles. The best defense against infantry remains the same as in World War I—the machine gun. Most modern battle tanks have two or three machine guns, with at least one of these pointing in the same direction as the main gun and operated from inside the tank with the hatches closed. Earlier tanks had machine guns mounted outside.

Support

Tanks need support vehicles. It is common practice to build a range of support vehicle bodies on top of the standard chassis (basic body shell) of an existing battle tank. These include bridge-laying tanks that have hydraulically operated folding bridges instead of turrets. These bridges can be rapidly placed across a river while under fire because the crew can do the job from inside the tank. Other variants include antiaircraft tanks and armored recovery vehicles with cranes.

The tank is the single most important fighting vehicle any army possesses. Advances in science, computers, metallurgy, and other technologies have revolutionized the accuracy and complexity of the systems onboard today's main battle tank.

> **See also:** GUIDANCE SYSTEM • GUN • INFRARED RADIATION • IRON AND STEEL • LASER • METAL • SUSPENSION

Tanker

A tanker is a giant cargo ship. Oil is pumped right into a tanker without being put in containers first. Tankers are enormous—the largest moving vehicles anywhere in the world. Some tankers are up to 440 yards (396 meters) long and can carry up to 500,000 tons (435,500 tonnes) of oil. Not all tankers carry oil; some carry cargo such as orange juice, wine, or molasses.

About two-thirds of the world's oil is transported from producers to refineries and user, by tankers. The vessels generally follow a fixed set of maritime routes. Not all of these routes can let the biggest tankers pass through. There is an optimum size of tanker for each route, taking into account the length of the voyage and the size of ports and any canals the ships have to negotiate.

Size

The first oil tanker, the *Gluckauf*, was built at Newcastle on Tyne, England, for a German owner in 1886. As more tankers were built through the years, they became larger; the more cargo a ship is able to carry, generally the cheaper it is to transport materials over long distances. However, size has its disadvantages, too. One limitation is the depth of water available to support the weight of the tanker. The larger the tanker, the deeper the water must be.

Most oil comes from the Middle East, so most tankers must travel through the Suez Canal. This waterway is relatively shallow, narrow, and difficult to navigate, so it puts limits on tanker size. However, from 1967 to 1975, the Suez Canal was

▶ *Tankers transport crude oil to refineries, where it is processed to make a variety of fuels, lubricants, gases, and chemicals. Tankers also transport many of these substances from refineries to customers in other countries. Oil tankers range in size from small coastal vessels 200 feet (60.6 meters) long, carrying about 2,000 tons (1,814 tonnes), to giant vessels that dwarf all other shipping.*

▲ *A tanker takes on oil at a floating terminal. Oil pumped from a nearby oil field is stored in tanks on the seabed. Floating terminals enable large tankers to be loaded safely in deep water without having to maneuver into a busy port or approach offshore oil platforms.*

closed to traffic. Tankers then had to go around the south of Africa to travel from the oilfields of the Middle East to Europe and North America. The waters on this route are deep, so the tankers could be much larger, and some big tankers were built during that period.

Tankers sailing between the Atlantic and Pacific oceans can use the Panama Canal to save themselves the long voyage around the southern tip of South America. The largest tankers that can pass through the canal are called Panamax vessels. A project to enlarge the canal so that two Panamax size vessels can pass each other in two-way traffic through the narrowest part, an 8-mile (13-kilometer) stretch called the Gaillard Cut, is currently under way.

The largest supertankers are called ultralarge crude carriers. Because of their size, special care must be taken to make them strong enough. Long ships tend to bend in rough seas and can even break

in two. To prevent this, they are divided into sections. Dividing walls running from the engine room (at the back of the vessel) to the bow split a tanker into several main sections. These sections are in turn divided into smaller tanks. The oil sloshing around in the tanks makes waves, and the force of the waves is cut down if the tanks are smaller.

Single and double hulls

Most oil tankers have a single hull; there is only one thickness of metal plate between the oil and the sea. When this is cracked or torn open in a collision, there is nothing to stop the oil inside from gushing out.

Following a series of major oil spills in the 1980s and 1990s, shipping authorities imposed new regulations banning single-hulled tankers from many ports and waters and requiring that new tankers be built with double hulls. Older tankers are also to be upgraded to a double-hull design. As its name suggests, a double-hull tanker has two hulls,

> ### DID YOU KNOW?
>
> The biggest oil tanker is the *Jahre Viking*. It is 1,504 feet (458 meters) long, 226 feet (69 meters) wide, and weighs 555,000 tons (503,385 tonnes).

one inside the other. The outer hull may be breached in an accident without damaging the inner hull, keeping the oil inside.

Controlling the tanker

It is very hard to stop a huge object like a tanker when it is traveling at full speed. It takes a long time for such a large mass to slow down. Navigating in busy or restricted waters is therefore difficult, and a sophisticated control system is needed. Nowadays, much of a tanker is computer-controlled, and only a small crew is needed to run it.

Loading and unloading

Again because of its size, the tanker cannot go into shallow coastal waters. So for loading and unloading, either a deep-water harbor is needed, or support tankers (which are much smaller) must transport the oil between the tanker and the shore. Sometimes the tanker uses floating terminals fed by storage tanks on the seabed—especially if the oil is from an offshore field.

The oil is pumped directly into the tanker from the well, refinery, or storage tanks. Care is needed in loading very large tankers—they must be kept balanced. If all the bow tanks were filled first, for example, the tanker would be heavily loaded at one

> ### DID YOU KNOW?
>
> The world's worst oil spill from a tanker occurred in 1979 when the *Atlantic Empress* collided with the *Aegean Captain* in the Caribbean Sea. A total of 35.5 million gallons (161.6 million liters) of oil was spilled into the sea.

end and could break in two. When it reaches its destination, the tanker uses its own pumps to remove the oil. This system is very fast and efficient—the tanker does not have to spend a long time in port, and costs are kept down.

Accidents

The effects of an oil tanker accident are usually disastrous. If a large tanker carrying oil sinks or is damaged at sea, the oil slick (oil spreading over the sea) will stretch for many miles, polluting the water and any shores it happens to reach. Fish and other sea life die, as do seabirds, whose feathers become matted with oil so that they are unable to fly. Oil slicks are very difficult to remove. Special chemicals have to be sprayed on the sea, and it takes a long time to clean up an oil-polluted coast.

◀ *An oil spill from a tanker can have a devastating effect on the environment and wildlife. When the Exxon Valdez ran aground in Prince William Sound, Alaska, in 1989, nearly 40,000 tons (36,280 tonnes) of oil was spilled. One-quarter of a million birds and thousands of other creatures, mainly sea otters and seals, are thought to have died as a result. A collision at sea may ignite the oil, and burning oil hampers any rescue attempts.*

▲ *Oil tankers are built from steel plate. New tankers are now built with double hulls for greater safety. The outer hull protects the inner hull that contains the oil.*

It is not only accidents that cause oil pollution. It is illegal to flush tanks at sea, but some tankers do, and this contributes to the world's pollution problems. If an explosion occurs due to the vapor left in empty tanks, which can happen while a tanker is in a harbor, there can be fire damage on a huge scale.

Future developments

In the late 1970s and early 1980s, most of the world was affected by an economic recession. One cause of this situation was the great increase in the price of oil charged by the oil states of the Middle East in the 1970s. Although oil has been found in other parts of the world (in the North Sea and Nigeria, for example), and the United States can meet most of its own needs, the Middle East is still the main source for the world as a whole. The Middle East is one of the world's most unstable regions. Wars and terrorism that threaten oil supplies can drive up oil prices on the world market and affect the economies in many countries.

Furthermore, people are becoming more concerned about the energy crisis and the probability that one day the world's supply of natural fuel will run out. Many countries are trying to cut down on fuel consumption. Meanwhile, other countries, such as China, that are experiencing rapid economic growth require increasing supplies of oil and materials made from oil to fuel their industrial development and satisfy their mushrooming demand for consumer goods.

Because oil tankers are constructed for carrying particular cargoes, they are actually very uneconomic. After they have delivered their cargo, they return to oil-producing countries with empty tanks. This practice is very expensive and wasteful.

To make better use of tankers, plans are being developed to adapt them to other roles. For example, tankers could carry oil from the Middle East, and on the way back carry water, which is much needed in that region. Other possibilities for returning tankers include carrying liquefied gas, or even acting as emergency aircraft carriers.

See also: NAVIGATION • OIL EXPLORATION AND REFINING • SHIP AND SHIPBUILDING

Taste

The delicious sweetness of a piece of chocolate cake, the tangy sourness of fresh grapefruit or apple juice, and the pleasant saltiness of potato chips are experienced through the sense of taste. Of course, the same sense makes a strong, bitter taste an unpleasant experience.

Taste is one of the five senses that humans possess to give them information about the world. Many people would say it is one of the most important because of the enjoyment it gives. Yet taste is the most limited of the senses. It tells people only if they like or dislike what they are eating and drinking. Even then, it is less important to the enjoyment of flavors than is the sense of smell.

When people try to describe foods they have eaten, they often use the words *sweet, sour, salty,* and *bitter.* The full flavor of food depends on its temperature, moistness, texture, and odor. If a pizza's doughy texture were changed by putting it into a blender and making it into a soupy mixture, the taste would not be the same at all. As for the aroma, its importance can be observed when a head cold prevents someone from smelling as well as usual. Food becomes tasteless without smell.

Taste buds

The sensation of taste comes through the taste buds, which are mostly on the tongue. Everyone has between 9,000 and 10,000 taste buds. They are mainly on the top of the tongue, inside bumps called papillae. Some are in other parts of the mouth and even in the throat. Half the taste buds are replaced every ten days through the body's system of constant renewal.

Different parts of the tongue deal with different tastes. The tip of the tongue tastes saltiness and sweetness, although sweetness is also tasted along a small area of the sides. The sides of the tongue react more strongly to sourness, and the back of the tongue gives the sensation of bitterness.

Taste is a crude, undeveloped sense in humans. Taste buds need 25,000 times more chemical particles to activate them than are needed to trigger the sense of smell.

▶ *Some people, with an especially well-developed sense of taste, are professional tasters of foods and drinks such as tea and coffee. Coffee tasters judge the quality of coffee by its aroma as well as by its taste, so they must also have a good sense of smell to do the job properly.*

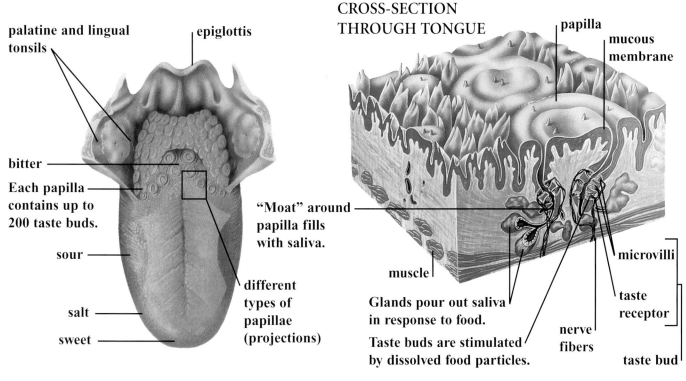

CROSS-SECTION THROUGH TONGUE

palatine and lingual tonsils

epiglottis

bitter

Each papilla contains up to 200 taste buds.

sour

salt

sweet

"Moat" around papilla fills with saliva.

different types of papillae (projections)

papilla

mucous membrane

muscle

Glands pour out saliva in response to food.

Taste buds are stimulated by dissolved food particles.

nerve fibers

microvilli

taste receptor

taste bud

▲ *The tongue is the main organ of taste, and different areas on it give the four different tastes. Bitterness is felt farthest back. Sweetness and saltiness are experienced on the tip. Sourness is tasted on the sides.*

Each taste bud has many cells with fine hairlike projections called microvilli. The microvilli come out through the small pores of the papillae. The taste buds are connected with the nerve endings in the tongue and tell the nerves nearest them to send impulses to the taste center of the brain. In other words, the taste buds pick up the chemical particles in food in the mouth and change them into nerve impulses, which are electrical messages. These impulses produce sensations of taste.

The chemicals in food must be in liquid form before they can be tasted. When food is chewed, saliva in the mouth dissolves these chemicals and turns them into a liquid. No one is sure exactly what happens to make the taste buds change the chemicals into nerve impulses, but it is believed that the chemicals change the electrical charge on the taste buds, which then causes the nerve to carry the message to the brain.

The brain

Messages about taste are taken to the brain by two nerves—the facial nerve and the glossopharyngeal nerve, which is connected to the tongue and the throat. These nerves take the message as far as the brain stem, where it is passed to specialized cells. The message is then sent to the other side of the brain stem and from there to the thalamus, which lies just above the midbrain. Then the nerve impulse is passed to the taste center of the cerebral cortex (the surface layer of the gray matter).

Problems with taste

People can lose their sense of taste if the facial nerve is damaged or if a head injury causes the loss of the sense of smell. Unpleasant tastes in the mouth are one of the signs of being upset emotionally. They are often very strong in cases of depression.

In the past, damage to the facial nerve was more common than it is today. It often happened during an operation for mastoiditis, which is a dangerous infection behind the ear. Antibiotic treatment has largely replaced this operation and so has reduced the possibility of damage to the facial nerve.

See also: BRAIN • FOOD TECHNOLOGY • NERVOUS SYSTEM • SMELL

Telecommunications

Telecommunications are vital to the modern world. Vast amounts of information are sent from place to place more quickly and cheaply than ever before. It is possible to pick up a phone and talk to someone thousands of miles away. Cell phones can be used to talk or send text messages. People can send copies of documents by fax and exchange messages using e-mail and the Internet.

Modern telecommunications evolved from experiments with electricity in the eighteenth century, when various people had shown that an electric impulse could be sent along a wire. Italian physicist Alessandro Volta (1745–1827) discovered electrical current and invented the battery, encouraging experiments in the transmission of electricity. Within a few years, various systems for sending messages over a distance had been tried.

Sending messages over long distances is called telegraphy. In 1836, English inventor William Cooke (1806–1879) saw a demonstration of a telegraphic device in Germany. He constructed several such devices himself, and then teamed up with English physicist Charles Wheatstone (1802–1875) when he learned he was working on the same project at King's College, Cambridge.

Cooke and Wheatstone's first instrument had six wires through which electrical impulses were sent to operate five needles. These needles turned to point to particular letters printed on a plate. Three years later, English engineer Isambard Kingdom Brunel (1806–1859) agreed to test their telegraph on the Great Western Railway, which he had built. It was put into operation to signal trains between London's Paddington Station and West Drayton Station, 13 miles (21 kilometers) away. In 1843, it was continued for another 7 miles (11 kilometers) to the station at Slough.

The chief use of the telegraph for many years that followed was for train signaling. The telegraph was an important safety improvement; before this time, the only way a train engineer could tell if another train was in the way was to lean out of the window and look.

At the same time, U.S. inventor Samuel Morse (1791–1872) was trying to get funds from the United States Congress for his telegraphic system,

▶ *Alexander Graham Bell's telephone was the star attraction at the American Centennial Exhibition in Philadelphia in 1876. It was hailed as "the greatest by far of all the marvels of the electric telegraph."*

which included a tapping code for the letters. In making his demonstration before Congress in 1844, Morse sent a message from Washington, D.C., to the city of Baltimore, Maryland, approximately 40 miles (65 kilometers) away.

Morse's system was simple and easy to install. It was based on the use of a single overhead wire, and the ground completed the electric circuit (path). An electromagnet in the receiver was activated by first making and then breaking this circuit. Clicking sounds were produced, and certain clicks were used to stand for certain letters, according to the code.

Wheatstone designed an automatic Morse system that used a punched paper tape. The message was first coded on tape and then sent at high speeds by an automatic transmitter that "read" the holes in the tape. Wheatstone's system could transmit up to 600 words per minute.

The Morse telegraph and Morse code spread very quickly. By 1852, there were about 40,000 miles (64,000 kilometers) of telegraph lines all over the world. Ten years later, there were telegraph lines across the entire continent of North America, and also from Britain to India. In 1866, the laying of a cable along the floor of the Atlantic Ocean made it possible to send telegraphic messages between Britain and North America.

Telephone

The telephone changes the spoken word into electrical pulses that can then be sent long distances along wires or by means of radio waves. International telephone calls now often travel by way of communications satellites thousands of miles above Earth.

The story of the development of the telephone is one of the most intriguing in the history of invention. Traditionally, Scottish-born scientist

▲ *A modern cell phone contains a circuit board carrying the electronic components that process, send, and receive callers' voices.*

Alexander Graham Bell (1847–1922) is credited as making the world's first telephone call, in March 1876 in Boston, Massachusetts. However, Italian inventor Antonio Meucci (1803–1889) almost certainly made the first call.

In the 1830s, working in Cuba, Meucci found that sounds could travel by electrical impulses through copper wire. He went on to develop some prototype telephones but could not afford a definitive patent for his designs. In 1860, Meucci successfully demonstrated his "teletrofono" in New York, and in 1871 filed a one-year renewable notice of an impending patent for his "talking telegraph." However, Meucci could not afford to renew the notice.

In 1876, Bell, who shared a laboratory with Meucci, filed a successful patent for a telephone. Later that year, Bell gave the first demonstration of his telephone to the American Academy of Arts and

DID YOU KNOW?

By 1866, the Western Union Telegraph Company had 75,000 miles (120,000 kilometers) of telegraph line in use.

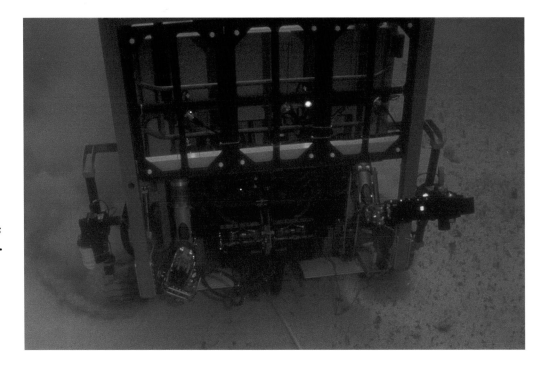

► *Intercontinental telephone cables are laid on the seabed by remote-controlled submersibles. On land, telephone cables are normally buried underground. Until the mid-twentieth century, telephone wires were strung between poles, still called telegraph poles, and from the poles to houses on every street.*

Sciences in Boston. Meucci sued Bell for stealing his invention, and fraud charges were started, but Meucci died before the case could be decided.

In 1877, Bell set up the world's first telephone company, the Bell Telephone System. The telephone took longer than the telegraph to be fully accepted and widely used. At first, it was used only for short-distance calls, the telegraph still being preferred for long-distance messages.

Since Bell's time, the telephone system has grown to cover the entire world and has expanded into space. When U.S. astronauts stepped onto the Moon, President Nixon congratulated them on the telephone. Telephones have changed a great deal since Bell's time. In recent years, telephones have been transformed by microchip technology. However, the principles behind the telephone have remained more or less unchanged over the years. A caller speaks into a mouthpiece and listens at an earpiece mounted together in a handheld device, a handset, or in a cradle looped over an earlobe.

DID YOU KNOW?

By 1885, there were 70,000 phones in people's homes all over the world.

The transmitter

The mouthpiece (transmitter) contains a microphone. Speaking into it makes a membrane vibrate. This in turn makes a wire coil vibrate next to a magnet. When a wire coil vibrates in a magnetic field, it makes an electric current flow in the wire. The electric current varies in step with the sound vibrations. Early telephones used carbon microphones. Speaking into a carbon microphone made a metal diaphragm vibrate. When it vibrated, it squeezed a container full of carbon granules. This changed the electrical resistance of the granules and varied an electric current flowing through them.

The receiver

This variable current travels along the telephone lines to the earpiece (receiver) of the person receiving the telephone call. The receiver acts like a miniature loudspeaker and converts the incoming electrical signals back into exact copies of the sound waves that originally entered the microphone of the caller at the other end of the telephone wires.

Making connections

Every telephone in a particular region is connected to other telephones through a telephone exchange. That telephone exchange is connected with others in the surrounding regions, forming a network that covers the country. For telephone transmissions abroad, calls are routed through local exchanges to international exchanges that are linked with exchanges in other countries. Practically all telephone exchanges these days work automatically, but human operators are on hand to offer assistance with difficult connections, interference on the line, and other problems.

To make a telephone call, the caller picks up the handset from its cradle. This closes the cradle switch connecting the telephone to the exchange and applies the line voltage. An automatic switching device or circuit then finds a spare line and applies the dial tone. The caller then taps the multidigit number of the person being called into the phone's keypad.

As the numbers are entered, the phone sends out the appropriate number of electrical pulses. In the older type of telephone exchange, connections between subscribers' lines are made by electromechanical equipment. They are electrical switches that move around and up and down, and are called selectors. An American undertaker named Almon Strowger (1839–1902) invented this type of mechanism in 1889.

A selector consists essentially of a contact arm mounted on a vertical shaft. This can move up and down between 10 levels. On each level, it can rotate and make contact with 10 equally spaced sets of contacts. When a number such as 2468 is dialed, for example, the pulses lift the contact arm of the first selector to the second level of contact. The arm then rotates and makes contact with the fourth contact. This connects with another selector, which moves to level 6 and then rotates to connect with contact 8.

This connects with the line of the subscriber being called. If the line is free, the exchange rings the subscriber's bell and applies a ringing tone to the caller's line. If the line is busy, the exchange applies a busy signal to the caller's line.

In most telephone exchanges these days, the Strowger mechanical system has been replaced by an electronic one. The switching is done

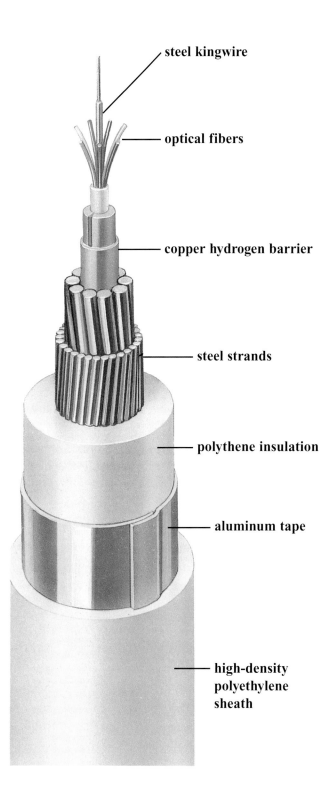

steel kingwire

optical fibers

copper hydrogen barrier

steel strands

polythene insulation

aluminum tape

high-density polyethylene sheath

▲ *A fiber-optic cable carries telephone calls as a modulated beam of light from a laser. A steel wire runs down the center of the cable to give it extra strength. Plastic sheathing protects the fibers from damage.*

▲ *Communications satellites circle Earth. Some are taken into space on space shuttles, as in this picture. Others are launched into orbit atop rockets. One satellite in space can replace hundreds of telephone relays on the ground.*

automatically by means of electronic microcircuits. It is considerably faster and more reliable than the earlier method.

Telephone lines

The connections between subscribers and local telephone exchanges are made by wire in much the same way as they were originally. But long-distance connections across the country and overseas may now also involve optical and microwave links, and communications satellites.

The subscriber/exchange links consist of pairs of small, insulated copper wires. Collected in large insulated cables, these connectors leave the exchange in underground pipes. The large cables branch off into successively smaller ones, which fan out to subscribers' houses. The trunk lines between exchanges must be able to handle large amounts of telephone traffic. Instead of being made up of pairs of wires, they are made up of coaxial cables. A coaxial cable consists essentially of a copper tube with a copper wire running down the middle. Cables like this can handle high-frequency signals, and the higher the frequency of transmission, the more "information" can be included in the signal.

The ordinary copper telephone cable is being replaced by fiber-optic cables. These consist of hairlike glass fibers, which have the ability to transmit light with very little loss to the outside. By using laser light, coded information can be sent

> ### DID YOU KNOW?
>
> The famous hotline that enables the U.S. president to speak to the Russian premier was established in 1984. Before that, there was a teleprinter link that transmitted printed messages.

through the fibers. The great advantage of this system is that, size for size, a glass-fiber cable can handle thousands of times more signal traffic than a copper cable can. Interconnection between glass-fiber cables, however, is more difficult.

Microwave links

In many areas the transmission of telephone signals now takes place through the air rather than cables. It is done by microwaves, radio waves between 1/25 inch (1 millimeter) and 12 inches (30 centimeters) long, equivalent to frequencies of 300 gigahertz to 1 gigahertz (1 gigahertz is 1,000 million waves per second). The microwaves are beamed in line of sight between tall relay towers. The signals are transmitted on carrier waves of microwave frequency, just as radio signals are carried on carrier waves of radio frequency.

For overseas telephone links, the microwave relay towers beam signals to a satellite ground station. From there a huge dish antenna beams up the

signals to a communications satellite in stationary orbit some 22,500 miles (36,000 kilometers) above the equator. In this location, it remains fixed relative to Earth. The communications satellite amplifies (strengthens) the signals and beams them back to another ground station. From there, the signals travel by microwave link and cable to the overseas subscriber. In 1988, the first fiber-optic telephone cable, called TAT-8, was laid under the Atlantic Ocean starting from Tuckerton, New Jersey. It is 4,114 miles (6,620 kilometers) long. It branches into two lines near Europe to serve both Britain and France. This cable could handle 37,500 simultaneous telephone calls.

◀ *Wireless access to the Internet is now possible without any physical connection to a telephone network.*

Going digital

Laying new cables is costly and only a limited number of frequencies are available, so engineers have tried to find ways of using a single cable for many telephone calls at the same time. This process is called multiplexing. Instead of sending the complete signal along the cable, the varying electrical signals are turned into numbers. This process is called digitizing. The strength of the signal is measured many thousands of times every second and converted into binary numbers consisting of just ones and zeroes. These numbers are represented by tiny pulses of electricity.

Numbers can be sent along a cable very rapidly and turned back into the original signal at their destination. The cable is used for only a very short period every few thousandths of a second for each call, so many thousands of separate calls can be combined and sent down one line. The calls are split up into lots of tiny "packets" of data, which are sent along the cable in the spaces between packets of other calls. At the other end, the various calls are reassembled and sent on to their destinations.

With multiplexed signals and optical fibers, the capacity of phone cables between major centers has increased many times over.

Compressing the data

Optical fiber cables link many main centers. But most telephones outside big cities are linked to the network by ordinary copper cables that may have been in place for decades. Engineers have found ways of squeezing more signals onto these cables,

too. A transmission system called Integrated Service Digital Network (ISDN) provides a raw data rate of 144,000 bits per second (bps). This is divided into two channels of data or voice at 64,000 bps, plus another channel of 16,000 bps for data or control signals. Another system, called Digital Subscriber Line (DSL), offers a fast, reliable connection that is increasingly popular for homes and small businesses. There are different types of DSL connections offering data speeds up to 16 megabits per second (mbps).

One type of DSL connection is known as ADSL. The "A" stands for "asymmetric," because data is received at a higher speed than it can be sent. This is suitable for Internet connections, because much more data is received than is sent. ADSL offers a connection speed up to 800 kilobits per second (kbps; transmit) and up to 8 megabits per second (receive). Data and voice can share the same line; a person can send e-mails while making a phone call. A filter connected to each telephone blocks the high-frequency data signal and lets the lower-frequency voice signal through to the telephone.

Mobile phones

Until the 1980s, nearly all telephones had to be connected to the public telephone network by a wire plugged into a wall socket. Telephones could not be moved around beyond the length of the wire. Mobile phones have no wire connection, so they can be carried anywhere. The first mobile phones were about as big and heavy as a toaster. Since then, their size has been reduced greatly.

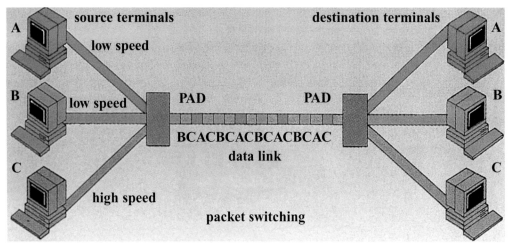

◀ *Data can be sent worldwide very cheaply by packet switching, which breaks down telephone calls into pieces called "packets." Each packet makes its own way through the network. At their destination, the packets are put back together in the right order. The line capacity is used more efficiently.*

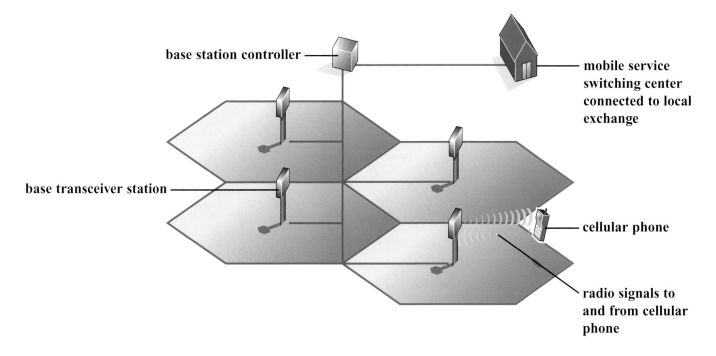

base station controller

mobile service switching center connected to local exchange

base transceiver station

cellular phone

radio signals to and from cellular phone

▲ *This illustration shows how a cellular phone system works. The system is so called because of the cell pattern into which the area covered is divided. A call from a mobile phone in a cell is routed through the cell's base station to another mobile phone in that network or to any other telephone, land-line or mobile, in another network. Not all cells are the same size. In a busy city, the cells may be as small as 300 feet (100 meters) across. In suburban and rural areas, where fewer calls need to be handled, the cells are bigger.*

A mobile phone is really a battery-powered telephone with its own radio transmitter and receiver. It is also called a cellular phone, or cell phone, because the region covered by the service is divided into smaller areas called cells. Each cell has a base station with an aerial for communicating with all the mobile phones in that cell. Adjacent cells use different radio frequencies to avoid interference. The same frequencies can be used over and over again in different cells as long as they are not used in adjacent cells.

When you switch a mobile phone on, it exchanges data with the base station so that the network knows where the phone is and which phone it is. The network needs to know this so that it can route calls to your phone. When you make a call, your voice is transmitted by radio to the base station, which sends it on to its destination. If you move from one cell to another, during a call, the network automatically switches your call to the base station in the new cell.

The first mobile phones were analog devices. Their main disadvantage was that anyone who tuned in to the right radio frequency could eavesdrop on private phone conversations. Cell phones of the next generation were digital and their signals were encrypted, or scrambled, so they were more secure. Digital compression techniques also enabled more data to be squeezed into the existing frequency bandwidth. Up to 10 digital mobile phone calls can occupy the same bandwidth as one analog call.

More and more features have been built into cell phones. Most have telephone directories, many have games, and some even have built-in digital cameras. All of the cell phones can send and receive text messages. Cell phones of the third generation have even more user features, including video messaging. Generally, the phones have been getting smaller, too.

See also: ELECTRICITY • ELECTRONICS • FIBER OPTICS • LASER • MICROELECTRONICS • OPTOELECTRONICS • SATELLITE

Telescope

A telescope is an instrument used for viewing distant objects. It has a system of lenses or mirrors that shows a greatly enlarged image of the objects being viewed. The most powerful telescopes are used by astronomers to study stars and galaxies millions of miles away.

▲ *Hans Lippershey, here in his workshop, probably invented the telescope, but Galileo perfected it. Early telescopes were small, because lens making was in its infancy. Even so, they gave astronomers a more detailed view of the Moon and planets than anyone had ever seen before.*

Dutch optician Hans Lippershey (1570–1619) began building crude telescopes in about 1608. In the following year, Italian scientist Galileo Galilei (1564–1642) produced a much better design and aimed it at the heavenly bodies. Galileo observed the mountains and craters on the Moon and the phases (changing appearance) of Venus. He also discovered four moons circling around Jupiter, now called the Galilean satellites.

Galileo built his telescope from a pair of lenses. The instrument was a type that scientists now call a refracting telescope or refractor. Galileo's refractor had a concave lens closest to the eye (called the eyepiece) and a convex lens at the far end (called the objective). This lens combination created a magnified image that was erect or correct side up. The same lens combination is used today in toy telescopes and opera glasses. These instruments have disadvantages: they cannot magnify to a great degree and have a narrow field of view.

The modern astronomical refractor has a different lens combination, with a convex eyepiece and a convex objective. It is called a Keplerian telescope, named for German astronomer Johannes Kepler (1571–1630). The double-convex lens combination produces better magnification and a wider field of view. It also produces an inverted (upside-down) image. These optical characteristics are unsuitable for terrestrial telescopes (for viewing on Earth), but they are perfectly acceptable for astronomical viewing.

The light-gathering ability of a telescope depends on the aperture (the diameter of the opening). It is difficult to build refractors in large sizes because of the problem of supporting the lens. This must be done from the sides so the supporting system does not get in the way of the incoming rays of light. Another disadvantage of refractors is that they suffer from lens defects, called aberrations, which cause distortion and color blurring.

Reflectors

It was to overcome the refractor's shortcomings that English scientist Isaac Newton (1642–1727) built a different type of telescope in 1668. Newton used a curved mirror to gather and focus the light. It was a reflecting telescope, or reflector. One of the most common types of modern reflectors still uses the mirror system that Newton devised.

In a Newtonian reflector, light gathered by the curved, concave mirror is reflected back up the telescope tube. Near the top of the tube the light is reflected through a right angle by a plane (flat) mirror inclined at 45 degrees. The light then enters an eyepiece at the side of the tube for viewing.

Another type of reflector, called a Cassegrain, was developed in 1672. It also has a second mirror near the top of the telescope tube. This time the mirror is curved (convex). It reflects light back down the tube through a hole in the main mirror and into the eyepiece. The Cassegrain reflector is more expensive to construct than the Newtonian reflector, so it is less used by amateur astronomers.

The reflecting telescope is also much easier to build in larger sizes because the light-gathering mirror can be supported from behind. Yet there is a limit to the size of mirror that can be made. One

▼ *A typical terrestrial telescope has a convex objective lens and can magnify images up to 60 times. This type of telescope has erecting lenses to make the image in the eyepiece appear the right way up.*

solution is to make the mirror in segments instead of one single mirror. The Multiple Mirror Telescope (MMT) on Mount Hopkins, Arizona, first had a main mirror made from six 72-inch- (1.8-meter-) diameter mirrors. Together, they worked like a single 176-inch- (4.5-meter-) diameter mirror.

When the MMT was built in 1979, it was impossible to make mirrors more than about 200 inches (5 meters) in diameter. Later, improved

A TERRESTRIAL TELESCOPE

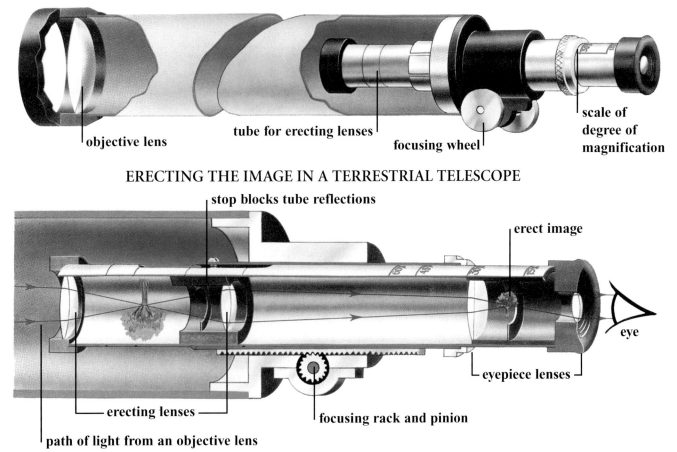

objective lens · tube for erecting lenses · focusing wheel · scale of degree of magnification

ERECTING THE IMAGE IN A TERRESTRIAL TELESCOPE

stop blocks tube reflections · erect image · eye · eyepiece lenses · erecting lenses · focusing rack and pinion · path of light from an objective lens

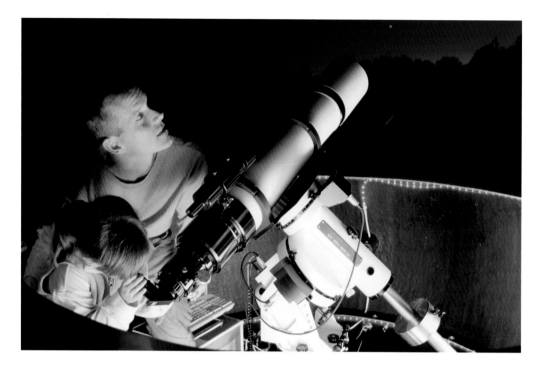

► *Amateur astronomy is a very popular pastime. Astronomy is one of the few branches of science in which amateurs can still make significant discoveries. Amateurs using telescopes regularly discover new comets.*

techniques made it possible to produce bigger mirrors. In 1996, the six mirrors in the Mount Hopkins observatory were replaced by a single 256-inch (6.5-meter) mirror.

These large lightweight mirrors consist of a thin reflecting surface over a honeycomb of glass ribs attached to a flat back plate. The honeycomb structure maintains stiffness while saving a lot of weight. Even lighter are meniscus mirrors—mirrors so thin that they cannot support their own weight. They are supported by an adjustable framework controlled by computer to keep the mirror in the perfect shape. The multiple-mirror technique is still used to make even bigger reflecting telescopes. Each of the twin Keck telescopes at the Mauna Kea Observatory in Hawaii has a 394-inch (10-meter) main mirror made from 36 separately controlled segments.

DID YOU KNOW?

A refracting telescope with an opening 40 inches (100 centimeters) across was installed at Yerkes Observatory in Wisconsin in 1897. It remains the world's largest refractor.

Different types of telescopes

Some telescopes are constructed to detect forms of electromagnetic radiation other than visible light. These include radio, infrared, ultraviolet, X-ray, and gamma-ray telescopes. The use of radio telescopes in particular has caused a revolution in astronomy over the past few decades.

Radio telescopes

A radio telescope is a device for collecting and recording radio waves from space. Almost all objects in the universe emit radio waves in addition to light waves. Radio telescopes help astronomers find out more about the universe than they could with optical telescopes alone.

Earth's atmosphere absorbs or reflects all radio waves apart from those with wavelengths between about 1.2 inches (3 centimeters) and 100 feet (30 meters), which can reach radio telescopes anywhere on the ground.

Objects in space emit tremendous amounts of energy at radio wavelengths. The signals are very weak by the time they reach Earth because they come from so very far away. All the energy collected by all radio telescopes since the beginning of radio astronomy is much less than the energy needed to light a flashlight for just a millionth of a second.

Start of radio astronomy

Radio waves from space were first detected by accident in 1932 by U.S. engineer Karl Jansky (1905–1950) at the Bell Telephone Laboratories in New Jersey. Jansky's job was to find the source of radio interference on long-distance telephone calls. Using a large trelliswork antenna that could be rotated on wheels, Jansky found that some static came from thunderstorms both nearby and far away. He also found a background hissing sound that turned out to be a constant stream of radio waves from the Milky Way galaxy.

Inspired by this discovery, U.S. amateur radio enthusiast Grote Reber (1911–2002) built a 31-foot- (9.4-meter-) wide bowl-like radio reflector in his backyard. This was the forerunner of the modern dish radio telescope. The dish reflected radio waves from the sky to a central focus point. There, Reber placed the antenna to detect radio waves from the region of the sky where the telescope was pointed. By moving the telescope about, Reber mapped radio waves coming from different parts of the sky. Reber alone pioneered radio astronomy during the years before World War II (1939–1945).

Radio telescopes are much larger than optical telescopes for two reasons. First, the incoming radio waves are so weak that a large collecting area is needed to gather them. A larger dish collects more radio waves and hence can detect fainter sources. Second, the larger the diameter of the reflecting dish, the smaller the details that can be seen. Radio waves have a much longer wavelength than light waves—typically one million times longer. Even the largest individual radio dishes cannot "see" the sky as clearly as the largest optical telescopes. The longer wavelength of radio waves means that the surface of a radio telescope's dish does not need to be as finely finished and smooth as the mirror of an optical telescope.

Observing with radio telescopes

Like any radio receiver, a radio telescope must be tuned to a particular wavelength—the frequency of the incident radiation. Many of the natural radio

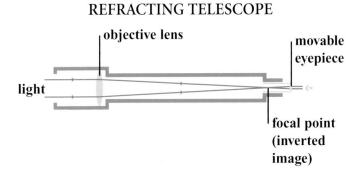

REFRACTING TELESCOPE

▲ *A refracting telescope produces a magnified image of a distant object by using lenses. Light enters through a convex objective lens. The light rays bend as they pass through the lens and they come together at the focal point. The image they form is magnified by a convex eyepiece lens.*

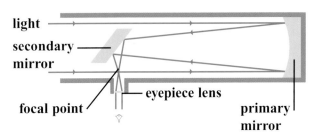

REFLECTING TELESCOPE

▲ *A reflecting telescope avoids some of the problems associated with refractors by using mirrors instead of lenses. Light entering a reflecting telescope is reflecting by a concave primary mirror, which bends the light rays toward a focal point. In this Newtonian reflector, a small flat mirror reflects the light out through the side of the telescope, where a convex eyepiece magnifies the image.*

sources in the sky emit radiation at all wavelengths. The radio astronomer can observe the same source in several different ways by tuning the receiver to different wavelengths. These observations can tell the radio astronomer much about the source, for example, whether the radio waves are coming from hot gas or are being emitted by electrons whirling around in magnetic fields.

Some of the cooler gases in space give out radio waves at specific wavelengths. The most important example is hydrogen, which emits at a wavelength of 8¼ inches (21 centimeters). A radio telescope tuned to this wavelength can therefore trace the

▶ *Large astronomical telescopes are usually built on mountaintops, as here at Mauna Kea, Hawaii. In the clean, thin air away from city lights, they "see" the clearest view of the sky. Mountaintop telescopes are usually housed inside a dome to protect them from the weather. The dome can rotate and doors open to let the telescope point at different parts of the sky.*

locations in space where hydrogen gas is concentrated. If the gas is moving with respect to Earth, the Doppler effect will make the wavelength slightly shorter or slightly longer than 8¼ inches (21 centimeters), depending on whether the gas is moving toward Earth or away from Earth. The slight change in wavelength is a measure of how fast the gas is moving.

In many regions of space, the gas atoms are combined in small molecules. In addition to hydrogen, the molecules contain atoms such as carbon, oxygen, and nitrogen, all of which are common in space. Each type of molecule gives out radio waves at a specific wavelength. So by tuning a

radio telescope to each wavelength in turn, a radio astronomer can readily determine which molecules are present in a given gas cloud.

Types of radio telescopes

After World War II, radio astronomy attracted large numbers of scientists who constructed radio telescopes with dishes that were much larger than the original one made by Grote Reber. One of the outstanding examples of the dish design is the colossal 250-foot (76-meter) radio telescope built by English scientist Bernard Lovell (born 1913) at

▼ *The Very Large Array in New Mexico is composed of 27 dish antennas, each 82 feet (25 meters) in diameter, on railway tracks. The positions and spacing of the dishes can be altered by moving them along the tracks.*

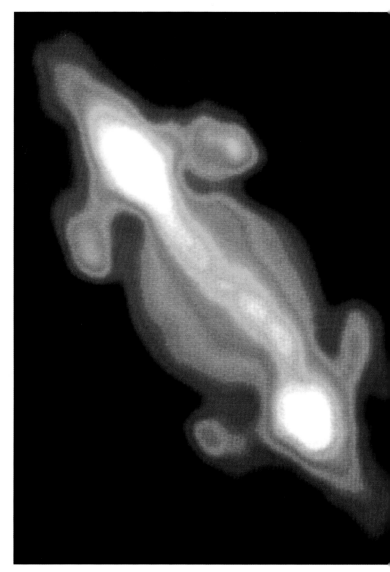

▶ *This is a radio image of radiation belts around the planet Jupiter. The pictures produced by radio telescopes have no color. Colors can be added to the pictures to show extra information. The different colors may show different intensities of radio energy or different velocities within a nebula or galaxy.*

Jodrell Bank near Manchester, England. This was the biggest radio telescope for 14 years until the 328-foot (100-meter) dish at Effelsberg, Germany, was completed in 1971.

The largest individual radio telescope dish of all is 1,000 feet (305 meters) across. The dish lies in a hollow between hills at Arecibo, Puerto Rico. It cannot be moved, but it scans the sky directly overhead as Earth rotates.

In Australia, astronomers developed a design known as the Mills Cross, which uses two long trough-shaped radio reflectors to study the sky. The Mills Cross is a type of telescope known as an interferometer. In this instrument, the output from two radio telescopes is combined to produce a more detailed view of the sky than would be visible from one telescope alone.

The combining of views has been carried to its limit by an imaging technique known as aperture synthesis. An aperture synthesis telescope is a long line of individual radio dishes all pointing at the same source. The signals received by all the dishes are combined in a computer. What comes out from the computer is a view of the sky that would be seen by one giant individual dish with an aperture the same as the length of the line of dishes.

The largest aperture synthesis radio telescope of all is the Very Large Array (VLA) outside Socorro, New Mexico. This radio telescope consists of 27 individual dishes arranged in a Y shape. It shows the sky in as much detail as would a single radio dish 22 miles (36 kilometers) in diameter.

Most exciting of all is the technique of very long baseline interferometry (VLBI). This system has two radio telescopes on different continents, several thousand miles apart, which observe the same source at the same time. The output from each is recorded. The two recordings are later combined electronically to show details of what was observed. The images produced using VLBI are a thousand times more detailed and clear than those seen through an optical telescope.

DID YOU KNOW?

Radio telescopes can transmit as well as receive signals. In 1974, the Arecibo radio telescope was used to transmit a message toward the M13 star cluster in the constellation of Hercules. The message will take about 24,000 years to reach the M13 cluster. If there is anyone there to receive the message, their reply will take another 24,000 years to come back to Earth.

Space telescopes

Telescopes designed to "see" radiation such as infrared, ultraviolet, X-rays, and gamma rays that are absorbed or reflected by the atmosphere are launched into space to orbit above the atmosphere. The United States launched a series of Orbiting Astronomical Observatories between 1966 and 1972. The last, OAO-3 (also called Copernicus) carried a reflecting telescope with a 32-inch (81-centimeter) mirror.

The International Ultraviolet Explorer (IUE) was launched in 1978 to study sources of ultraviolet radiation. The Infrared Astronomical Satellite (IRAS) made the first infrared study of the universe in 1983. Exosat studied X-rays between 1983 and 1986. The Compton Gamma Ray Observatory was launched in 1991 to study gamma rays. The Chandra X-ray telescope was launched in 1999 to study X-ray sources.

The Spitzer Space Telescope was launched in 2003. It makes images from the infrared (heat) rays emitted by objects. The 33½-inch (85-centimeter) telescope can see through clouds of dust and gas and reveal objects that are normally hidden within them and behind them. It can also detect cool stars and planets orbiting other stars.

These are just a few examples of the many telescopes that have been launched since the 1960s. The biggest space telescope launched so far is the Hubble Space Telescope (HST), named for the U.S. astronomer Edwin Hubble (1898–1953). It was launched from the Space Shuttle *Discovery* in 1990. It measures 43 feet (13 meters) long by 13.8 feet (4.2 meters) wide and weighs 24,000 pounds (11,000 kilograms). It resembles a large trash can with wings—the wings being a pair of solar panels that generate electricity.

Soon after the HST was launched, astronomers discovered that it could not be focused to produce sharp images. A tiny error of just one-fiftieth the width of a human hair had been made in the shape of the main mirror, but that was enough to blur the telescope's vision. The space shuttle returned to the telescope in 1993, and astronauts fitted optics designed to correct the error. With its "sight" corrected, the HST could distinguish objects as small as a dime at a distance of 12½ miles (20 kilometers). Since then, the HST has taken

▶ *The Hubble Space Telescope orbits 355 miles (569 kilometers) above Earth and is operated by remote control by astronomers on the ground. Light enters the narrow end of the telescope and travels down to the 94-inch (240-centimeter) primary mirror. This reflects the light to a small 12-inch (30 centimeter) secondary mirror. The light bounces off this mirror and travels down through a hole in the middle of the primary mirror to a series of instruments and cameras.*

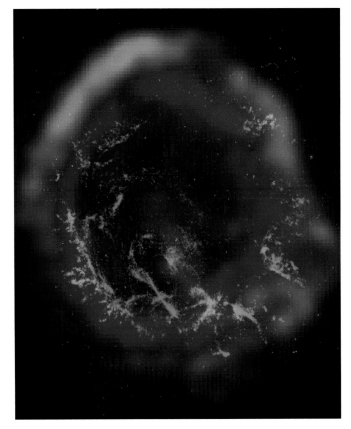

▶ *This composite image shows a supernova remnant as seen by an optical telescope (green color), X-ray telescope (blue), and radio telescope (red).*

thousands of spectacular photographs of distant galaxies, nebulas (vast clouds of gas and dust), star clusters, and supernovas (exploding stars).

The instruments that use the light collected by the telescope are located behind the main mirror. Some of them simply take pictures; others analyze the light; and others are used for measuring the exact positions of objects under study. One of these devices is the wide-field camera, which uses electronic sensors known as charge-coupled devices (CCDs) to take pictures of the sky.

The CCDs are far more sensitive than a normal photographic plate and so can record much fainter objects than can conventional photography. Many terrestrial telescopes have been updated and improved by adding CCD-based imaging systems. A second, similar device known as the planetary camera takes more detailed electronic pictures of smaller regions of sky, such as the surface of a planet and its moons or rings.

A particularly valuable detector, built by European scientists, is the faint-object camera. It uses electronic techniques to intensify light collected by the space telescope. In this way, the faintest objects, such as galaxies in the farthest reaches of the universe, can be seen.

Two other devices are known as spectrographs. These spread out the light from objects in space so that astronomers can analyze light of different wavelengths. Spectrograph studies reveal the make-up of the objects being viewed and provide clues to the physical processes going on, such as high-speed motions of gases. Another device, called a photometer, measures the brightness of objects in space. It can detect the rapid flashing that might happen, for example, in hot gas that is swirling around a black hole.

Finally, the space telescope has three guidance sensors that keep it pointing accurately at the target. These sensors lock onto guide stars and ensure that the telescope is precisely maneuvered. The entire 11-ton (10-tonne) telescope will point

with an accuracy of 0.007 seconds of arc, which is the apparent size of a period seen at a distance of 6 miles (10 kilometers). One of the guidance sensors will be used to measure the exact positions of stars.

Future space telescopes

The next space telescopes are now being designed and built. The Next Generation Space Telescope (NGST) has a mirror more than twice as wide as the HST's mirror. Large mirrors are difficult to construct, so the NGST's mirror is made from 18 separate segments. The telescope will be positioned about 1 million miles (1.6 million kilometers) from Earth. It is designed to operate at a temperature of about −400°F (−240°C), so it is fitted with a sunshield to stop solar radiation from heating it up. The James Webb Telescope will take over from the Hubble Space Telescope from about 2011.

See also: ASTRONOMY • DOPPLER EFFECT • OBSERVATORY • RADAR • RADIO • SOLAR SYSTEM • SPACE SHUTTLE • STAR • UNIVERSE

Television

The television has transformed society since the first model was developed in the 1930s. The television provides a window on the world that entertains and shapes our beliefs and ideas. There is a television in almost every home, yet most people do not really understand how it works.

The word *television* means "viewing from afar." The development of the television was largely due to the work of Scottish engineer John Logie Baird (1888–1946), but there were many other pioneers in this field, including British engineer A. A. Campbell Swinton (1863–1930) and Russian-born U.S. scientist Vladimir Zworykin (1899–1982). John Logie Baird made his invention public in January 1926, and between 1929 and 1935, he transmitted television pictures using the medium-wave transmitters of the British Broadcasting Corporation (BBC), although not many people had television sets to watch them.

As early as 1884, however, German inventor Paul Nipkow (1860–1940) had taken out a patent for a machine that sent pictures, but he could not make a commercial success of his invention. More than 40 years passed before U.S. inventor C. F. Jenkins (1867–1934) and John Logie Baird, in Britain, gave successful demonstrations of television. Only two years later, in 1928, Vladimir Zworykin produced a fully electronic system of television broadcasting. Zworykin also invented a scanning tube used as the television screen. He called the camera tube an iconoscope, from the Greek words *icon*, meaning

"image," and *scopon*, meaning "to observe." Zworykin's devices revolutionized television, and gradually the early problems began to be solved.

Baird's system was of low definition—it had only 30 lines, so the screen was not able to show the sort of detail that can be seen in a photograph or on a movie screen. The BBC began regular television broadcasts in 1936, not with Baird's system, but with a rival electronic system that produced 405-line pictures, which, of course, were in black and white.

Early home television sets had a screen size of 5 inches (12.5 centimeters) across. Screen size grew to 9 inches (23 centimeters) by about 1939. All of these early sets used a great deal of power, so much of the later work on television went into making the picture larger and the working parts smaller. By the late 1950s, home screens of 19 and 21 inches (48 and 53 centimeters) had become fairly common.

The transistor was invented in the United States in 1948 by engineers John Bardeen (1908–1991), Walter H. Brattain (1902–1987), and William Shockley (1910–1989). It was not widely used in electronic equipment for about ten years. In the 1960s, transistors replaced vacuum tubes in television sets. Later, even more compact integrated circuits, or chips, replaced individual transistors.

▶ *This plasma television screen produces a bright, high-quality picture because it works in a similar way to a fluorescent light tube. Instead of producing white light, as the fluorescent tube does, a plasma screen produces millions of tiny spots of red, green, and blue light that merge together to form the picture.*

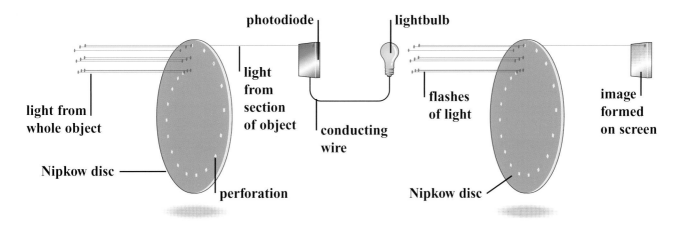

▲ *This illustration shows the main components of a mechanical scanning system. An opaque wheel with a spiral of holes, called a Nipkow disc, spins in front of the image. As each hole passes in front of the image, it reveals one line of the image. The following hole reveals another line below it, and so on. This process converts the image into a series of lines. The light passing through the holes in the disk strikes a light-sensitive device such as a photoelectric cell or photodiode. This changes the light into an electrical current, which varies in strength in step with the light. This electrical current varies the intensity of light from a bulb. The bulb shines through a second Nipkow disc and projects a copy of the original image on a screen.*

Color television was developed rapidly in the United States, where the first color broadcasting service began in January 1954. Now, television is available around the world. With the development of satellites in space, it is possible to watch the news in other parts of the world as it happens. The first transatlantic transmission by satellite was in July 1962 between Andover, Maine, and Pleumeur-Bodou, France, via the satellite Telstar 1.

The television camera

The process of how a picture reaches a television is very complicated. The first stage in this complex process is the creation of an image of the scene to be televised. Light from the scene is focused by the zoom lens of the television camera. A set of prisms and mirrors inside the camera splits the light into three separate beams. One contains all the red information in the picture, one represents the blue information, and the third is the green part of the picture. Each beam strikes a different light detector.

The light detector in early television cameras was a glass tube containing a light-sensitive screen called a signal plate. Light falling on the signal plate changed the amount of electricity that could pass through it. An electron beam scanned the signal plate, swinging back and forth like a person's eyes following the lines of text on a page. The beam could pass through the brighter parts of the plate more easily than darker parts. Thus, the pattern of light on the signal plate was converted into a pattern of electricity. A black-and-white camera had one tube; a color camera had three.

In modern television cameras, the light detectors are charge-coupled devices, or CCDs. CCDs are smaller and more robust than glass tubes, and they form sharper pictures.

DID YOU KNOW?

U.S. inventor Philo Farnsworth (1906–1971) conceived the basic requirements for a television system while he was still in school. He successfully transmitted a television picture in 1927. Farnsworth went on to hold some 165 patents for cathode-ray tubes, scanners, devices to convert an optical image to an electrical signal, and many others.

As light hits a CCD, it falls on a grid of light-sensitive components called photodiodes. Photodiodes conduct tiny amounts of electricity when light falls on them. The electricity is stored on the chip. Therefore, the pattern of light hitting a CCD creates a similar pattern of electric charges all over the CCD. The camera "reads" these charges, point by point, row by row, to create a signal that can be broadcast and used to form a picture on a television screen.

The color television system used in the United States (known as NTSC—National Television System Committee) uses a color coder to process the red, blue, and green picture signals. They are turned into a luminance (brightness) signal and two chrominance (color and density) signals. Only the luminance signal is picked up by a traditional black-and-white receiver.

Broadcasting

There are basically two methods by which the output of a television camera reaches the receiver. In the first method, the signal is carried directly by line. This method is known as closed circuit television (CCTV), and it is widely used for education, scientific research, medicine, commerce and security. In industry, CCTV enables processes to be watched at points where it would be inconvenient or dangerous for a human observer to

HOW A TELEVISION PICTURE IS FORMED

go, for example, in the reactor room of a nuclear power station. Traffic control can be made easier by mounting television cameras at important points and watching the traffic flow from a central control room.

In security, a closed circuit system can enable a single person to watch the whole floor area of a large department store by switching between several cameras. Prison guards also use cameras to survey the outer walls.

Television can also be distributed to people's homes by cable. Cable television can provide additional programs for entertainment or education and allows direct communication between viewer and station in a two-way process.

In the second output and receiving method, the signal is transmitted by means of radio waves. Transmitting radio and television over a wide area is also called broadcasting. Radio waves are made up of electric and magnetic fields that alternate as they travel through the atmosphere at the speed of light. They may be used to carry information. The picture signal from a camera is transmitted by adding it to a radio signal called a carrier wave.

◀ *A television picture on a cathode-ray tube is formed from a series of lines. An electron beam scans the screen from side to side and also moves down the screen, building up the picture line by line. Variations in the intensity of the electron beam vary the brightness of the spot on the screen struck by the beam. A color television creates a color picture in the same way, but with three electron beams, each creating a different color on the screen: red, green, and blue. A close look at a television set will show both the lines and the colored dots or strips.*

▶ *This illustration shows how a picture tube works. Three electron beams are fired at the screen: red, blue, and green. The strength of the beams varies according to the strength of light in the original scene. The beams activate phosphor dots or strips on the back of the screen, and they are guided by a shadow mask or aperture grille, a plate that consists of a fine network of holes or slots. Strong beams will make the phosphor glow brightly, but a weak beam will cause less reaction. In this way, the different tones of the original scene are faithfully reproduced in the television image.*

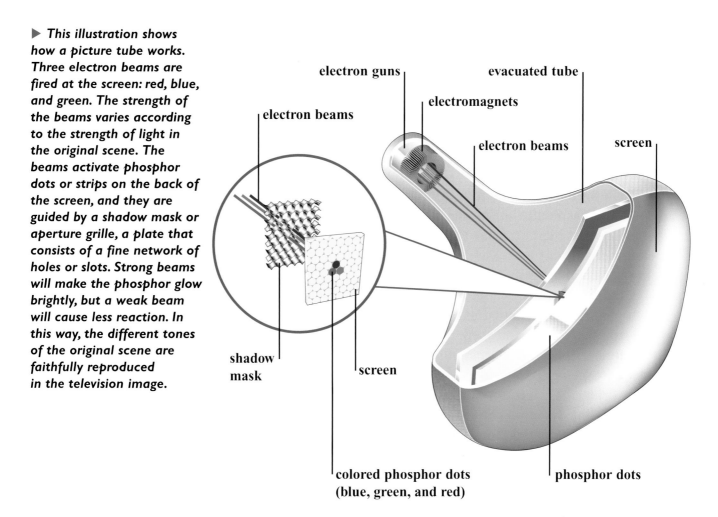

electron guns

evacuated tube

electromagnets

electron beams

electron beams

screen

shadow mask

screen

colored phosphor dots
(blue, green, and red)

phosphor dots

Adding the picture signal to a carrier wave changes, or modulates, the carrier. In the NTSC system, the carrier is modulated by another carrier wave (the subcarrier), which carries the two chrominance signals. The whole package, including the visuals and synchronizing signals (to keep reception in time with transmission) and the sound carrier waves as well, is broadcast from an antenna tall enough so waves can travel clear of obstructions.

DID YOU KNOW?

Color television had been proposed as long ago as 1904. John Logie Baird was the first person who successfully demonstrated color television, at his studios in London on July 3, 1928.

Receiving

The signal from the broadcasting antenna is picked up by home television antennae that are connected to home television sets by a cable. When a set is switched on, its tuner picks out one particular video signal. Changing its tuning selects different signals for different channels. The sound signal is separated and amplified (made stronger), and then a loudspeaker converts it into sound waves.

In color sets, the picture signal is split into three separate color signals once again—red, blue, and green. These signals are also amplified and fed into three electron guns at the back of the picture tube. They fire beams of electrons at the screen, one for each color, red, blue, and green. The signals control the amount of electricity that leaves the guns and strikes the phosphor dots on the back of the screen. A strong electric beam makes a phosphor color glow brightly, and a weak beam makes the color

▶ *This picture shows a magnified section of a liquid crystal display (LCD). The screen consists of a pair of glass plates with tiny squares of liquid crystal material between them. When electrodes on the glass plates are charged with electricity, the crystals twist. This twisting motion is used to block light or let it pass through the screen. By using colored filters, each spot on the screen can be made to glow red, green, or blue.*

glow dimly. The beams scan the screen from side to side and build up the picture line by line. The more scan lines a picture is built up from, the higher the definition—the amount of clear detail in the picture. In the United States, 525 lines are used and 30 pictures are transmitted per second. To avoid flicker, each picture is transmitted in two halves— all the odd-numbered lines and then all the even-numbered lines. Displaying alternate lines in this way is called interlacing. Each half-picture is called a field; two fields make up a whole picture, or frame. The 625-line system—known as PAL (an acronym for phase alternating lines)—common in Europe, transmits 50 fields, or 25 frames, per second. This transmission is comparable to movie film, which displays 24 pictures per second.

Behind the television screen is a metal plate called a shadow mask or grille. It has thousands of holes or slots that ensure that the beams of electrons are directed to the correct colors. The front of the picture tube is the screen, known as the face plate. The image on the screen is made up of very tiny red, green, and blue dots or strips. By looking very closely at a television screen, it is possible to see these.

The red, blue, and green dots combine to make up a complete picture. All other colors can be made from combinations of these three primary colors. In fact, the television works on the same principle as color printing. If a photograph in a magazine is examined under a magnifying glass, exactly the same effect made by color dots can be seen.

◀ *In a television studio, the pictures from several cameras are fed to a control room, where a director chooses which picture is broadcast or recorded on video for later broadcast.*

camera 1

The dotted line shows the shot the camera is taking of this scene.

camera 2

The picture that appears on viewers' television screens.

▲ *These illustrations show how color separation overlay (CSO) works. CSO is very useful for trick effects. One camera points at people or objects in front of a blue screen. A second camera points at a completely different background. At every point where blue is detected in the first image, the corresponding point of the second image is substituted. Using this technique, people in a television studio may appear to be in a field, in a city thousands of miles away, or even on the Moon.*

It is possible to see the individual lines that make up the television screen image. They correspond exactly to the grid pattern on the CCD in the camera and can be seen more easily on a black-and-white set than on a color set.

In effect, a television picture is a tiny spot of light flashing incredibly rapidly across the screen, line by line, over and over again. The picture is built up gradually, in the same way that an artist moves a pencil quickly over paper to create a sketch. It takes only 52-millionths of a second to flash across one line. This movement is too fast for the human eye to notice. Any image that the human brain receives through the eyes takes one-tenth of a second to fade, an effect known as persistence of vision. When we watch a movie, the sequence of frames in the film gives the illusion of movement. In the same way, the television signal seems to our eyes to present a smooth, natural sequence of action.

Microchip technology

The arrival of the microchip has changed the designs of television sets a great deal. The old, bulky sets, which took several minutes to warm up, are today a thing of the past. Portable and miniature television sets are now common.

Microchip technology enables extra features and services to be made available. Not all of the 525 (or 625) lines transmitted to a television are used to produce a picture. The spare lines are used to carry extra information. Viewers can select from hundreds of pages of information in text form, ranging from news, sports, and weather reports to travel information and television program schedules. Each page has its own number, which is selected by keying it into the television set's remote control handset.

Video recording

The development of videotaping has also changed the face of television. It is used in the studio to record programs for later transmission and by the public to record programs. Pre-recorded video tapes of movies are rapidly being replaced by the digital versatile disc (DVD), a disc that looks like a compact disc (CD) for music but stores a whole movie and more. Recordable DVDs already enable people to record television programs on discs. There are also some home recorders that are based on computer hard disk technology.

Small to large sets

With continuing advances in electronics, television manufacturers keep devising improved and different ways for people to view their favorite programs. Television enthusiasts now have

▶ By using a video telephone, such as the one pictured here, people making a telephone call can see each other as well as hear each other.

choices that range from a giant 35-inch (89-centimeter) direct-view color television receiver or projection screen, to slim, pocket-sized sets that do not use the usual picture tubes, with all kinds of variations in between.

For people on the move, there are handy television sets small enough to fit in a coat pocket. Instead of bulky picture tubes, they have flat liquid crystal display (LCD) screens that are only about ⅛ inch (3 millimeters) thick. Some cellular phones with color LCD screens can now show television pictures, too.

The plasma screen is another alternative to the traditional cathode-ray tube. Plasma screens are thin enough to hang on the wall, like a picture. A plasma is a gas made from charged atoms, called ions, and electrons. A plasma screen is made from a pair of glass plates with hundreds of thousands of tiny spaces, called cells, between them. The cells are filled with the gases xenon and neon. One set of long electrodes (metal contacts) are mounted on the back glass, and another set is mounted on the front plate. One set runs from side to side, and the other runs from top to bottom, so they cross each other and form a grid. This matches the grid pattern on the camera CCD.

When the two electrodes are charged with electricity, the gas in the cell at the point where they cross is changed to plasma, which emits invisible ultraviolet radiation. This excites a phosphor material coating the inside of the cell. There are three phosphors that glow red, green, and blue. The color of each point in a picture, called a pixel, is produced by a group of red, green, and blue cells. The degree to which each cell

▶ *The vehicle in this picture contains an onboard television set. Car manufacturers are experimenting with onboard televisions that can display pictures from a DVD player. A DVD stores images and sound as a pattern of pits in the surface of a reflective disc. As the disc spins in the player, a laser points at it. As the pits pass beneath the laser beam, they produce a flickering reflection. This is converted to a varying electric current, which a television set recognizes as a television signal.*

is charged with electricity determines how brightly its red, green, or blue phosphor glows, creating different colors.

Digital television

When television began, it was an analog medium. The signal transmitted varied in strength or frequency in proportion to the information it carried. The main drawback of analog television is that any impairment of the signal, caused by bad weather or reflections from nearby buildings, also impairs the quality of the picture received. Digital television eliminates these problems.

In a digital television system, the picture information is converted into a coded series of pulses before transmission. It is the code that contains the picture information, not the size or frequency of the signal. So, even if the signal is impaired or degraded a little, a perfect picture still appears on the screen as long as the code can be detected. A decoder in the television set, or in a separate box, reads the code and uses it to produce the signal that creates the picture.

Satellite television

Television was traditionally broadcast from transmitters on top of tall towers. A receiving antenna has to be in the direct "line of sight" of the transmitter to receive a signal. Obstacles such as hills, trees, or tall apartment buildings can block the signal between the transmitter and receiving antenna. Making the transmitter towers several times taller would solve this problem, but this is not a practical solution.

Satellite television is really a method for placing television transmitters high above the ground without building very tall towers. Television satellites are placed in orbit 22,500 miles (36,000 kilometers) above Earth. At this height, a satellite orbits Earth in exactly the same time as Earth takes to turn on its axis, so the satellite stays above the same spot on Earth's surface all the time. A dish antenna receiving signals from the satellite therefore does not have to be steered or adjusted. It can be fixed in one position.

Television programs are transmitted up to a satellite, which receives them and rebroadcasts them down to the ground. To receive the programs, a small metal dish is pointed at the satellite. It concentrates the radio signals onto a detector, called a low noise block (LNB) down-converter held above the dish, which passes the signals down a cable to a receiver. The receiver decodes the signals and converts them into pictures and sound.

DID YOU KNOW?

A television satellite has to fly through space at a speed of about 7,000 miles (11,000 kilometers) per hour to keep up with the turning Earth.

See also: ANTENNA • CABLE TELEVISION • COMMUNICATIONS SATELLITE • ELECTROMAGNETISM • SATELLITE

Temperature

Temperature indicates how hot or cold an object is. It is usually measured with a thermometer, which is a device with numbered marks called a scale.

Everything in the universe consists of tiny particles called atoms. In most cases, atoms are bound to other atoms by chemical bonds to form molecules. Molecules and the atoms from which they are made are moving constantly. As a gas, molecules move freely and rapidly until they collide with other molecules. As a solid, the molecules are restricted to vibrating about their equilibrium positions. Motion in liquids involves a combination of vibration and free motion over short distances.

Temperature scales need fixed points to be useful. The usual fixed points are those at which water changes from solid to liquid (melting or freezing point) and from liquid to gas (boiling or condensation point) at standard atmospheric pressure.

Melting occurs when the molecules in a solid begin to move freely and not just vibrate around their average positions. Freezing occurs in a liquid as energy is removed so that the forces between molecules prevent any free motion. The freezing point and melting point of a pure substance are the same. In a liquid, the molecules have enough energy to move with respect to each other but not to separate fully. When the average energy allows molecules to enter the gas phase, its temperature has reached the boiling point.

Temperature scales

On the Fahrenheit (F) temperature scale, the freezing point of water is taken to be 32°F, while the boiling point of water is 212°F. Thus there are 180 degrees Fahrenheit between the freezing and boiling points of water.

▶ When moisture freezes in the atmosphere, it can form complicated branching flakes. When these flakes fall on frozen ground, they form a carpet of snow. The snow lies permanently above an imaginary line called the snowline.

▲ Only a few plants and animals can survive in very hot places, as here in Monument Valley, Arizona. The highest temperatures on Earth are reached in the sandy desert regions of the United States, North Africa, and Australia.

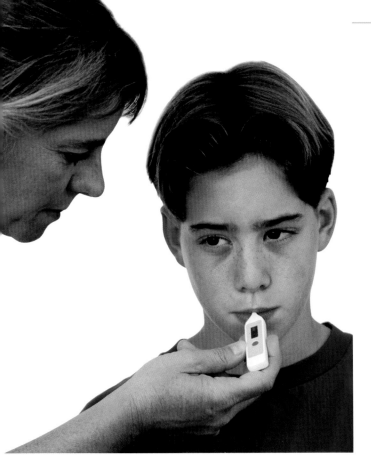

even metals. For example, iron melts at 2795°F (1535°C) and boils at 5072°F (2800°C). Gold melts at 1947°F (1064°C) and boils at 5085°F (2807°C).

Triple point

The temperature and pressure at which a substance can exist as a solid, liquid, and vapor together is called the triple point. The triple point of water is at a temperature of 273.16K (32.02°F or 0.01°C) and a pressure of 0.09 pounds per square inch (0.015 kilograms per square centimeter). At this temperature and pressure, water can exist as ice, liquid water, and water vapor at the same time.

Temperature extremes

Temperatures on Earth's surface range from as low as −129°F (−89°C) in Antarctica to as high as 136°F (58°C) in Libya. The hottest planet in the solar system is Venus. The temperature on its surface has been measured at up to 900°F (482°C), which is hot enough to melt lead. The boiling point of a liquid is dependent on air pressure. Raising the pressure also raises the boiling point. The thick, high-pressure atmosphere on Venus would raise the boiling point of water to about 300°F (150°C).

Absolute zero

There seems to be no upper limit on the temperature that can be reached. However, there does seem to be a lower limit. This limit is called absolute zero, and on the Kelvin temperature scale it is 0K. Absolute zero is equivalent to −459.67°F or −273.15°C. According to the laws of thermodynamics, absolute zero can never be reached. The lowest temperature so far recorded is half a millionth of 1K.

On the centigrade (Celsius) temperature scale, there are 100 degrees between the freezing and boiling points of pure water. The freezing point is 0°C, and the boiling point is 100°C.

A third temperature scale—widely used by scientists—is the Kelvin thermodynamic scale of temperature. It is named for English scientist William Thomson (later Lord Kelvin; 1824–1907). On this scale, there are no negative temperatures. The freezing point of fresh water on this scale is 273.15K; and the boiling point, 373.15K. Similar to the Centigrade (Celsius) scale, there are 100 degrees between the freezing and boiling points of water, so an interval of one degree kelvin is the same as an interval of one degree centigrade (Celsius). Temperatures on the Kelvin scale can be converted to centigrade (Celsius) by subtracting 273.15. There have been other temperature scales. On the Réamur scale, named for French scientist René Réamur (1683–1757), water froze at 0°R and boiled at 80°R.

Water exists as a liquid and a vapor over most of Earth's surface. Other materials are normally solid on Earth's surface, but if they are heated enough, they have their own melting and boiling points—

See also: HEAT • MEASUREMENT • THERMOGRAPHY • THERMOMETER

Tesla coil

Croatian-born U.S. physicist Nikola Tesla (1856–1943) started his scientific career in Paris, France, but emigrated to the United States in 1884. He worked on a number of projects, including transformers, dynamos, and electric lightbulbs. Tesla is particularly remembered for the coil apparatus that takes his name. The Tesla coil is used to generate very high-voltage and high-frequency currents.

▲ *In this picture, artificial lightning is generated in Tesla's laboratory. Great care must be taken in designing, making, and using Tesla coils, because of the high voltages and great power involved in their use.*

When Tesla arrived in the United States, he went to work for the U.S. inventor Thomas Edison (1847–1931). While Edison favored direct current (DC) electricity, the sort of electricity produced by a battery, and worked by trial and error, Tesla found alternating current (AC) more interesting and calculated everything in great detail before starting work. Inevitably, these differences in working methods led to arguments between the two scientists. Within a year, Tesla left Edison's laboratory and set up his own laboratory. One of his most famous inventions was the Tesla coil, which he invented in 1891.

When Tesla demonstrated his coil, it produced voltages of up to 100 million volts and sent fountains of electric arcs (sparks) showering across the room. The electric arcs act like lightning. They break down the air and form a substance called ozone, which has a distinctive smell. The sound, light, and smell produced by a Tesla coil in action made it a spectacular experience.

Tesla experimented with increasingly bigger coils and coils made in different shapes. He started with ordinary cylindrical coils and then made cone-shaped coils and flat helix- (spiral-) shaped coils.

A Tesla coil produces intense electric fields. A fluorescent tube held in such an electric field will illuminate, even though no wires are connected to

it. The biggest and most powerful Tesla coils can light fluorescent tubes up to 50 feet (15 meters) away. Tesla used this effect to light his own laboratory. A loop around the ceiling was always energized. If a part of the laboratory needed more light, all that was necessary was to place a tube there, and it would light up.

How does a Tesla coil work?

The Tesla coil may be set up with other electrical apparatus to form either of the circuits illustrated on the facing page. In the first type of circuit (see the first illustration), an induction coil is used to increase the voltage provided by the electrical source. The induction coil is formed from two coils and an iron core. The primary (inner) coil consists of only a few turns, but the secondary (outer) coil has many turns. Changes in the supply of current to the primary coil induce (create) a high voltage in the secondary coil.

The high-voltage terminals (electrical connectors) of the induction coil's secondary winding form a gap across which an electric spark runs when the circuit is activated. This circuit is

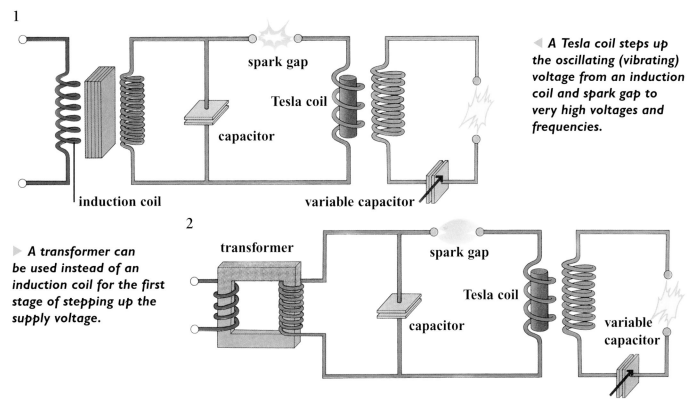

1

spark gap

Tesla coil

capacitor

induction coil

variable capacitor

◄ *A Tesla coil steps up the oscillating (vibrating) voltage from an induction coil and spark gap to very high voltages and frequencies.*

▶ *A transformer can be used instead of an induction coil for the first stage of stepping up the supply voltage.*

2

transformer

spark gap

Tesla coil

capacitor

variable capacitor

completed through a capacitor (a device for storing an electric charge) and the primary winding of the Tesla coil. This primary winding consists of a few turns around a nonmagnetic core. It is separated by air or oil from the multiple turns of the Tesla coil's secondary winding. This causes the voltage in the Tesla coil's secondary winding to be stepped up yet again. The spark gap in the first circuit causes the current in the primary winding of the Tesla coil to oscillate (vary) at a high frequency, and this is passed on to the secondary winding. A variable capacitor may be included in the secondary circuit to make it resonate with the primary circuit—that is, to increase the oscillations in the current. The Tesla coil can therefore produce very high voltages and high frequencies.

Tesla tuned his coils to different electrical frequencies in the same way that tuning forks are tuned to different musical pitches. A coil tuned to one frequency energizes other coils tuned to the same frequency simply by being near them. The second illustration above shows an alternative arrangement in which the original voltage is stepped up by a transformer instead of an induction coil.

Radio and television

Tesla coils are used in systems that need high voltages and high frequencies, such as radio and television circuits. A modified type of Tesla coil, called a flyback transformer, produces the very high voltages needed to power a traditional television set with a cathode-ray tube.

◄ *Tesla coils, invented in 1891, are still used today in some radio and television circuits.*

See *also:* CAPACITOR • ELECTRICITY • INDUCTION • TRANSFORMER

Textile

The manufacture of textiles has a long history and owes as much to early handicrafts as to scientific invention. Although modern textiles are mainly used to make clothing, soft furnishings, and carpets, they also have an increasingly diverse range of uses in industry. Fabrics of any kind are called textiles and are generally made through processes such as weaving, knitting, and bonding.

Early peoples soon recognized the possibilities presented by natural fibers such as cotton, linen, wool, and silk. Ancient Peruvians used cotton to make clothing and tapestries as early as 8000 BCE, with production later developing in China, India, and the Middle East. Cotton has remained the most widely used natural fabric.

For thousands of years, humans have taken the fleece of sheep to make wool for use in clothing or carpets. The earliest fragment of carpet discovered dates from 500 BCE and was found perfectly preserved in an ice-filled tomb in the Altai Mountains of Russia. This remnant of a Persian carpet was made using the method that remains the most common for making handmade rugs, called Ghiordes knots.

Silk is the most expensive natural fiber and has been produced in China for five thousand years. It is made from silkworms that feed on mulberry trees. The "worms" are the larvae, or caterpillars, of a moth. Each larva spins a protective cocoon of fine silk thread about 900 feet (275 meters) long. The Egyptians, meanwhile, were among the first to produce the coarser fabric linen, which was used for wrapping mummies. Linen, silk, and cotton were all introduced to Europe by the Romans.

Cloth was also dyed and printed from very early times. Evidence of this process has been found in the Roman ruins of the second century BCE. There are also indications that printed textiles were produced in India during the fourth century BCE.

Weaving yarn

The main methods of production are weaving, knitting, and spinning, and they also originated thousands of years ago. Weaving involves interlacing strands of fibers called threads or yarns on a simple device called a loom. First established in the Stone Age, weaving developed in both North and

◀ *Throughout the developing world, textiles are still made by hand on small looms.*

▶ *Fashion stores are filled with clothes of a wide variety of fabrics such as handmade and machine-made natural and artificial fibers, which are often printed and embroidered with decorative designs.*

South America during prehistoric times. The simple looms used in Egypt as early as 4400 BCE share similarities with those used by Navajo and Southeast Asian weavers today.

On a typical loom, long threads (the warp) are meshed with others at a right angle (the weft) to make a fabric. The three stages of weaving are known as shedding, picking, and beating in.

Shedding involves separating the warp into two sets of threads using harnesses. One of the harnesses is raised to elevate a set of threads. The space between is called the shed. The second stage, called picking, involves placing a strand of weft yarn between the sets of warp yarn, and then the harness swaps position. The weft yarn is now clasped between the warp threads. In beating in, a moving bar pushes the freshly inserted weft yarn into position along the edge of the woven cloth. The sequence is repeated until the fabric is complete.

Spinning and knitting

Spinning involves twisting fibers around one another to form a continuous yarn. Spinning was originally done by hand using tools called a distaff and spindle. These were replaced by the spinning wheel, which was invented in India and introduced throughout Europe during the Middle Ages. This invention helped create a more uniform yarn. The user simply held the yarn in one hand, feeding it onto the wheel as it spun in the opposite direction.

Hand knitting originated among the nomads of the Arabian Desert around 1000 BCE, and it gradually spread to Europe. Knitting guilds were established in Paris and Florence during the Middle Ages. The basis for modern commercial knitting equipment was established in 1589 with the development of a frame-knitting machine.

Royal influence often led to the production of fine textiles in Europe. Elaborate silk fabrics with gold threads, for example, were made in palace workshops in Sicily, Italy, in 827 CE. Following a French conquest, the weavers fled to Lucca, Italy.

◀ *Threads or yarns are colored with natural or artificial dyes. The variety of hues and shades is almost infinite.*

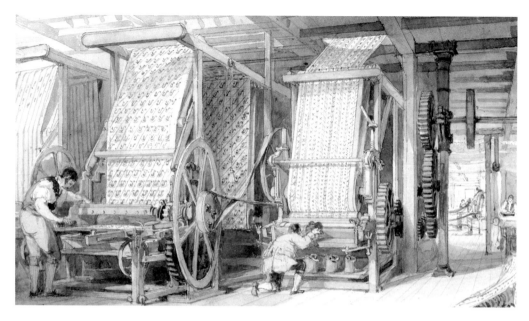

▶ *This interior view of a cotton mill in 1834 shows workers printing long rolls of calico, which is a simple woven cotton fabric that originated in Calicut, India. The invention of textile machinery revolutionized cotton manufacturing.*

The town became a center for fine woolens, employing more than 45,000 workers by the end of the fifteenth century.

Birth of an industry

Producing cloth now played a large part in the wealth of nations. In the sixteenth century, a lucrative velvet industry started to flourish in Venice and Genoa in Italy. The French manufacture of woven silks began at the end of the fifteenth century. In 1520, under the direction of King Francis I (1494–1547), Flemish and Italian weavers were brought to Lyon, France. Lyon would become the center of European silk manufacture.

Between the thirteenth and eighteenth centuries, few changes were made either to the loom or the spinning wheel. For centuries, the textile industry remained a cottage industry, meaning that work was usually undertaken at home. This was certainly the case in England, where huge numbers of textile workers owned either a loom or spinning wheel, or both. But a series of very important inventions in England in the eighteenth century led to the start of mechanization in the textiles industry.

Mechanization and the growth of factories

By 1730, weavers started to use a shuttle for weaving. This handheld device enabled fabric manufacture of a maximum width of 30 inches (75 centimeters). Use of the shuttle required great care and only slightly increased the speed of work. In 1733, English inventor John Kay (1704–1764) improved on this design with his flying shuttle, allowing the user to pull a cord, which made the shuttle move back and forth automatically in a quick, jerking motion. This cheap machine doubled the speed of weaving and allowed the yarn to be wound off more easily.

English weaver James Hargreaves (1720–1778) created a machine called the spinning jenny in the 1760s, capable of spinning as many as eight threads simultaneously. A disadvantage of the spinning jenny was that the thread produced was weak and only suitable for use as weft.

Spinning jenny to power loom

Soon afterward, English industrialist Richard Arkwright (1732–1792) improved on the spinning jenny to produce a machine that gave the thread a twist as it was pushed through rollers, making it strong enough for use as both weft and warp. Most significantly, the water frame, powered by a flow of water from a river or stream, signaled the start of the factory age. Technology became still more advanced in 1779 when British inventor Samuel Crompton (1753–1827) introduced the spinning mule, a combination of the spinning jenny and the water frame.

DID YOU KNOW?

Textiles have increasingly innovative uses in industry. The manufacture of airships and balloons uses a blend of synthetic fibers and strengthened natural fabrics. The military requires special clothing that can protect soldiers from severe weather conditions and purchases textiles in the form of tents, inflatable life vests, and parachutes. Astronauts, on the other hand, require spacesuits that are strong enough to withstand extremes of both air pressure and temperature. The transportation industry uses fabric in car seats, seat belts, and air bags. Hospitals use cotton textiles to make bandages and dressings, while polyester is used in replacement joints and arteries and also in surgical stitches.

The spinning mule was superseded once again in 1785 when clergyman Edmund Cartwright (1743–1823) invented the power loom, which was a weaving machine that could be powered by a horse, waterwheel, or steam engine. Cartwright even made a device to stop the loom immediately if the weft thread broke or ran out or if the shuttle became stuck.

The power loom could produce fabric three or four times faster than a skilled weaver using traditional methods and has been called the parent of the modern loom. As a result, wages dropped and fear of unemployment grew.

From the introduction of the flying shuttle, workers felt angry about inventions that seemed to threaten their existence. Known as the machine breakers, these workers were determined to prevent the rise of innovations. The machine breakers destroyed a number of Hargreaves's machines, and they attacked the mills using the power loom. A hostile crowd even attacked John Kay, who fled to France where he later died in poverty.

Factories and productivity

The burgeoning factory system produced a leap in national productivity but brought great misery for employees. Children formed a large percentage of the workforce, often working in excess of 12 hours each day for low pay. The early machines could not be stopped in an emergency, and therefore a momentary loss of concentration could prove fatal.

◄ *Traditionally, cloth for clothes was cut by hand. With mass production came mechanized cutting machines. Lasers are now used to cut through many layers of cloth at a time.*

Children were often at the greatest risk because they were employed for dangerous tasks involving moving around the machines while in use.

In the nineteenth century, further developments saw productivity continue to rise, linked to a drop in the cost of textile products. By the twentieth century, improvements were linked with increasing understanding of the chemical properties of fibers rather than engineering modifications.

Artificial fibers

The introduction of artificial fibers was among the most significant advances in the textiles industry. Rayon, an artificial silk, was one of the first synthetic fibers and was developed by the chemical modification of a substance called cellulose, which is derived from wood pulp.

The crucial discovery that chemicals derived from coal and oil could help make fibers led to the manufacture of nylon in 1937, followed shortly after by polyester and acrylic. These synthetic fibers tend to be cheaper to manufacture because they require less preparation.

The blending of synthetic and natural fibers has produced improvements to textiles. Combining polyester with silk or cotton, for example, makes garments less prone to creasing. Acrylic, which is soft and warm, can be mixed with wool to create cheaper knitwear. Nylon is often mixed with wool to create low-cost carpets.

Today, most countries have factories capable of highly efficient fabric production. Most processing is done by machine, but many mills still employ some hand production. Modern industrial looms are entirely automated. Electronic sensors help guarantee an even weave by identifying when there is too much tension in the warp. These machines are huge, and the shuttling action makes them very noisy. The most recent modification has been to convey the weft yarn on a jet of water or air instead of using a device for weft insertion.

Hand looms are only used to make specialized fabrics. Harris tweed, for example, is a patterned woollen textile produced in Scotland using a loom controlled by a foot pedal. These looms are better engineered than the old power looms, but they are otherwise very similar.

Special effects and textures

Modern spinning is also mechanized. The fibers, called slivers, are fed into machines to make them longer and thinner. Spindles twist the fibers to hold them together and make the yarn stronger. The twisting process can be used to produce different style finishes, such as a crinkling effect.

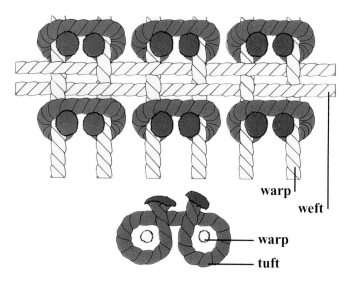

▲ *This illustration shows the Ghiordes or Turkish knot, which is used in handwoven Oriental rugs. Pairs of tufts are pulled through between the warp threads.*

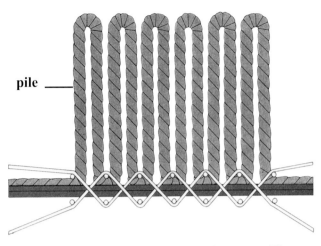

▲ *This illustration shows the Brussels weave. This type of weave was started in France and Belgium. The loops of the pile are formed over rods.*

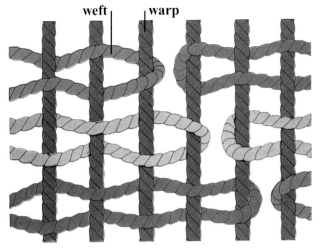

▲ *The Turkish kilim rug is woven like tapestry. The designs are formed by the weft colors, which are doubled back where a color ends.*

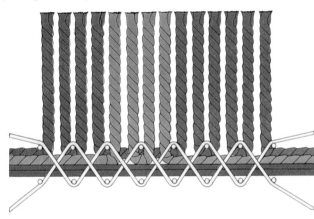

▲ *The Wilton carpet replaced the Brussels weave but uses the same weave. The loops are cut into tufts by blades that replace the rods.*

▲ *This illustration shows the Axminster carpet. In this weave, the tufts are inserted individually. Different colors are pulled through by pincher-like grippers.*

Industrial knitting machines produce fabric with the same structure as knitting by hand but with far greater efficiency. The machines create warm woollen garments and make lace from cotton and hosiery from wool, silk, or nylon.

Some fabrics, such as felt, are made by bonding fibers together using adhesives or stitching. Unlike woven fabrics, felt does not fray when it is cut. Because felt lacks the same strength, it is typically limited to making clothing lining and toys.

After manufacture, various finishing treatments are applied to modify the fabric's surface. These can serve to make items more practical by making them crease- or shrink-resistant. Wool and silk fabrics can be coated with the chemical naphthalene to make them mothproof. Flame retardant chemicals are often used in home furnishings and children's clothing. Alternatively, a finish can be applied to make fabric more attractive. A process called calendering makes the surface very smooth and shiny by passing fabric through heated rollers to melt strands together.

Machines are used for automatic quality testing and can assess fibers, yarn, and fabric properties. Yarns are tested for uniform thickness, and the fastness of the finish is also assessed. Some manufacturers attach trademarks or quality labels as guarantees.

See also: COTTON • DYE AND DYEING • FIBER • WOOL

Thermoelectricity

A thermoelectric device changes heat into electricity or electricity into heat. These devices are used in certain types of thermometers, refrigerators, and small power generators.

The term *thermoelectricity* is used to describe three effects: the Seebeck, Peltier, and Thomson effects. The Seebeck effect can be seen when two different metals are joined to make an electrical circuit. If the two places where the metals meet are kept at different temperatures, an electrical current will flow in the circuit. The Peltier effect is the opposite of the Seebeck effect. When a current is driven around a circuit that contains two different metals, one junction (where the metals meet) will heat up and the other junction will cool down. The Thomson effect occurs in a metal that is not the same temperature all over. When a current is passed along a metal bar, heat can be taken in or sent out so the temperature along the bar changes.

The Seebeck effect

In 1821, German physicist Thomas J. Seebeck (1770–1831) discovered the effect named for him using bismuth and copper wires. The effect can also be seen in any two metals or even in two samples of the same metal if they contain significantly different amounts of impurities.

Metals are good conductors because metal atoms are surrounded by a "sea" of negatively charged particles called electrons that are free to move along the metal. It is this movement of electrons that makes an electrical current.

The number of free electrons in a metal depends on the type of metal and the temperature of the metal. The hotter it is, the more electrons are free to move along it, and the faster they can move. Two different metals will have different amounts of electrons available to move. When these metals are joined, the faster-moving electrons in one metal will progressively drift into the other metal.

Before the electrons move from one metal to the other, both metals carry no spare charge. The number of negative electrons balance the number of positive nuclei (particles at the centers of atoms) in the metal. After the electrons have moved, there is an imbalance in electrical charge. This produces an electric field across the meeting point that will increase as the temperature of the junction is changed.

If two wires of different metals are joined to form a loop, this pairing is called a couple. There are two junctions in the circuit. When the metals in the

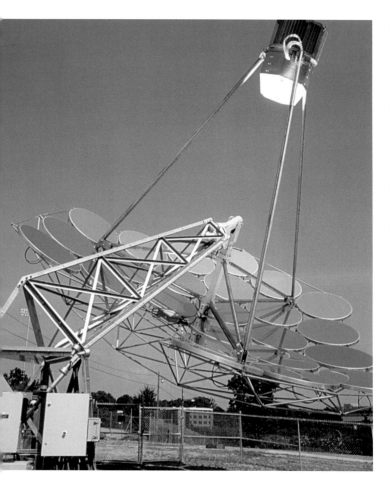

◀ *This solar power generator comprises a dish-shaped reflector that directs sunlight onto a thermoelectric device suspended above it. The heat of the Sun's radiation is converted into electricity.*

▶ *A thermoelectric generator onboard the* **Cassini** *spacecraft is prepared for testing. Similar devices are used by the military. Some military thermoelectric generators are fitted to vehicles, where they use the engine exhaust to heat one side of the device and engine coolant to cool the other side.*

couple are at the same temperature, the voltage across one junction cancels out the opposite voltage across the other, and no current flows. When the junctions are at different temperatures, current does flow. This phenomenon is the Seebeck effect.

The Peltier effect

The Peltier effect is named for French scientist Jean Peltier (1785–1845). When a current is forced to flow around a couple, one junction gets hotter, and the other becomes cooler. When the current travels around the couple, it meets an electric field at one junction that is like a downward slope, called a voltage gradient. The current can "fall down" this slope easily. At the other junction, the current must climb up the voltage gradient.

The Thomson effect

If a current is made to flow in a metal bar that is not the same temperature all over, heat is either sent out or taken in. The effect is named for Scottish physicist William Thomson (later Lord Kelvin; 1824–1907). The change in temperature across the bar is called a temperature gradient, and this temperature gradient produces an electric field or voltage gradient in the metal.

Thermocouples

Thermocouples make use of the Seebeck effect. The voltage that is induced, known as the electromotive force, is very small. As the temperature difference between the junctions is gradually increased, the electromotive force increases in step. At a certain temperature, called the neutral temperature, the electromotive force suddenly stops increasing. If the temperature difference continues to increase, the electromotive force will actually drop back to zero and then begin to increase in the opposite direction at the same rate.

Thermocouples can be connected in series, when they are called thermopiles. Thermocouples and thermopiles are used in industry for measuring temperature differences.

Some space probes are powered by small thermoelectric generators. The *Galileo* probe to Jupiter and the *Cassini* probe to Saturn had thermoelectric generators that used plutonium-238 as their heat source.

See also: ELECTRICITY • GENERATOR • KELVIN, LORD • METAL • SPACE PROBE • TEMPERATURE • THERMOMETER

Thermography

Every object, including the human body, gives off rays of heat that cannot be seen by the naked eye. These heat rays can be changed into colors that can be seen. Heat "pictures" are very useful in medicine, and they can even help people to see in the dark.

Thermography is a process used to produce images of the heat on the surface of the body. Warmer parts of the body show up in different colors from cooler areas. These pictures, called thermograms, guide doctors to unhealthy areas of the body. Thermography is also used to make heat pictures of the surface of Earth, which are useful to scientists and sometimes the military.

All objects give off heat rays called infrared radiation, even when they are at low temperatures. The amount of radiation increases as the temperature of the surface rises, and it is also affected by the type of surface. For example, rough black surfaces give off significantly more heat than smooth, shiny black surfaces.

Infrared radiation cannot be seen by the naked eye, but it can be detected by thermographic sensors. An infrared camera or scanner picks up the heat energy and makes a thermogram. This pattern of heat can then be shown as an image on a television or computer monitor.

The colors of the thermogram correspond to different temperatures. Usually red colors show higher temperatures than blue colors. This map of color consists of hundreds and thousands of separate temperature measurements.

Thermography in medicine

The temperature of diseased tissue is often higher than that of the surrounding healthy tissue. The unusual temperatures may be caused by changes in blood flow just under the skin, or by changes in the

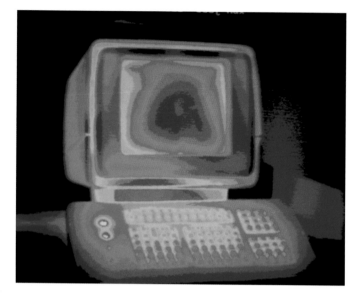

▲ This thermogram of a computer and keyboard shows the warmest parts in orange and yellow and the coolest in blue.

cells below the skin. The temperature difference can be readily detected by thermography. The heat pattern of a healthy person is usually the same on both sides of the body. A growth in the body, such as a tumor, needs extra blood, which raises the temperature of the nearby skin. This warmer skin will show up on a thermogram in colors different from the other side of the body and thus reveal a diseased area.

Thermography is important for detecting breast cancer at an early stage. It is also used for examining burns without disturbing the victims. Diseases of the arteries and veins are also often revealed through the use of thermography.

Measuring the body

Thermography takes place in a room that is kept at a cool and constant temperature. The body of the person being examined is uncovered and rested in the cool room for about ten minutes. Because heat radiation travels through the air, there is no contact between the individual and the machine. No metal touches the skin to upset the temperature readings, and no form of radiation reaches the patient.

▶ A technician aims a thermovision camera at a patient's hands to diagnose hand disorders. A computer screen (on the right) reveals the thermogram of the patient's hands. The image is color-coded by temperature; black shows the coolest areas, and green shows the hottest areas.

Night into day

Infrared radiation can be used to see in the dark, so it is useful for undercover surveillance work and security systems. A filter converts white light into a beam of infrared light. The infrared beam cannot be seen unless a person looks through a viewer or wears goggles. Infrared light cannot be seen, so people do not normally know that they are being observed. However, it is easy to carry a detector that gives a warning if any infrared light is present.

Analyzing photographs

Infrared photographs are very useful when taken from the air, as they provide views that could not be seen otherwise. Film that is sensitive to infrared light is used in the camera. After the film has been developed, it is printed as a normal photograph.

Vegetation, such as a treetop, reflects infrared radiation. Vegetation that is alive and healthy shows up as red or pink, while other objects stand out as blue. Pollution in rivers and lakes similarly reflects more infrared radiation than clean water.

Hot engines

Thermal imagers are devices that detect the heat patterns from buildings, vehicles, and people. The imagers make use of infrared radiation to build up a thermogram on a screen. A truck, for example, will be displayed on the screen as a warm engine and transmission, with a cooler body. People are shown with warm faces and hands, contrasted with cooler clothing. Aircraft or vehicles can be identified after they have left the area because they leave behind a thermal pattern on the ground.

◀ Rescuers use thermal imagers to search for people in smoke-filled rooms during a fire. Thermal imagers can also be used to locate people buried in collapsed buildings after an earthquake by looking for the heat of their bodies.

See also: INFRARED RADIATION

Glossary

Aberration In optical lenses, a fault in an image occurring because of the shape of the lens (spherical aberration) or because of an alteration in color (chromatic aberration).

Absolute zero The lowest possible theoretical temperature limit, measured on the Kelvin scale as 0K (−459.67°F or −273.15°C).

Allotrope One or more forms of an element that differ in physical, and often chemical, properties.

Auroras The dramatic visual displays seen in the sky at the North and South poles, which are caused by the interaction of the solar wind with Earth's magnetic field.

Ballast Heavy materials, such as stones or lead, put in the holds of ships to keep them stable.

Black hole A region of space in which the pull of gravity is so strong that nothing, not even light, can escape from it.

Condensation Change of physical state from a vapor to a liquid.

Constellation Group of stars that can be seen in a particular part of the night sky.

Corona Outermost layer of the Sun's atmosphere that becomes visible only during total solar eclipses.

Damping Progressive decrease in the amplitude of an oscillation or vibration due to the expenditure of energy by friction, viscosity, or other means.

Electromagnet An iron core with wires wound around it that operates as a magnet only when an electrical current is passed through the wire.

Laser A device that generates an intense beam of pure electromagnetic radiation, which can, among other things, be used to cut through metal, perform eye surgery, and carry telephone conversations.

Light-year The distance light travels in a vacuum in one year—approximately 5.88 trillion miles, or 9.46 trillion kilometers.

Mean An average value of a set of values, which is expressed as the sum total of the set of values divided by the number of values.

Median A value in an ordered set of values above and below which there is an equal number of values; also, the arithmetic mean of the two middle values when there is no middle number.

Meniscus The curved upper surface of a column of liquid.

Mode The most frequent value in a set of values.

Nebula A gas cloud in space generally composed of hydrogen and organic molecules. Star formation occurs in nebulas when the gas conglomerates.

Neutron star Extremely compact, dense star composed almost entirely of neutrons.

Nova Stars that suddenly increase in brightness by roughly a thousandfold.

Parsec An astronomical measurement of distance equivalent to 3.5 light-years.

Prism In optics, a transparent solid used to produce or analyze a continuous spectrum.

Red giant Large, cool star that shines brightly with a reddish light.

Sunspot Large, cool patch with a strong magnetic field, visible on the surface of the Sun.

Supernova Rare stellar outburst during which a star increases in brightness by roughly a millionfold.

Thryistor A semiconductor device that acts like a current-controlled switch.

Triangulation A method in surveying that enables the accurate measurement of a distance between any two points.

Vacuum A space entirely devoid of matter, or more generally, a space that has been exhausted to a high degree by an air pump or other artificial means.

Vaporization Change of physical state from a liquid to a vapor.

Vulcanization The process of treating crude or synthetic rubber with chemicals, such as sulfur, to give it useful properties, such as elasticity.

White dwarf Dense, hot star that has exhausted nearly all its available energy and has shrunk to a size roughly equal to that of Earth.

Index

Page numbers in **bold** refer to main articles; those in *italics* refer to illustrations.